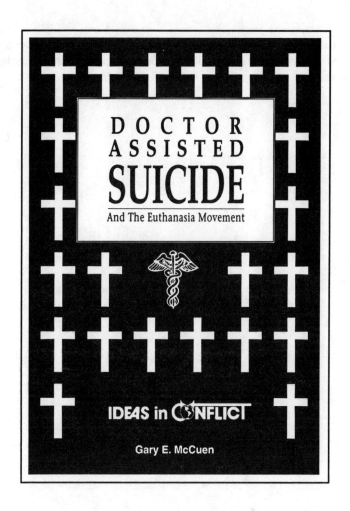

DOCTOR ASSISTED SUICIDE

And The Euthanasia Movement

IDEAS in CONFLICT

Gary E. McCuen

411 Mallalieu Drive
Hudson, Wisconsin 54016
Phone (715) 386-7113

Illustration and Photo Credits

Tony Auth 162, 163; Steve Bensen 68; Darren Brettingen 31; Craig MacIntosh 11, 25, 103, 157; Gary Markstein 47; Eleanor Mill 152; Mike Ramirez 135; Steve Sack 95; Bill Schorr 127; David Seavey 17, 43, 63, 79, 85, 113, 119, 141; Wayne Stayskal 37; Tom Toles 73; Richard Wright 147.

GEM
GARY McCUEN
publications inc.

© 1994 by Gary E. McCuen Publications, Inc.
411 Mallalieu Drive, Hudson, Wisconsin 54016

(715) 386-7113

International Standard Book Number
ISBN 0-86596-093-3
Printed in the United States of America

CONTENTS

Chapter 3 EUTHANASIA IN THE NETHERLANDS

Chapter 4 PHYSICIAN-ASSISTED SUICIDE: IDEAS IN CONFLICT

REASONING SKILL DEVELOPMENT

These activities may be used as individualized study guides for
students in libraries and resource centers or as discussion catalysts
in small group and classroom discussions.

This series features ideas in conflict on political, social, and moral issues. It presents counterpoints, debates, opinions, commentary, and analysis for use in libraries and classrooms. Each title in the series uses one or more of the following basic elements:

Introductions *that present an issue overview giving historic background and/or a description of the controversy.*

Counterpoints *and debates carefully chosen from publications, books, and position papers on the political right and left to help librarians and teachers respond to requests that treatment of public issues be fair and balanced.*

Symposiums *and forums that go beyond debates that can polarize and oversimplify. These present commentary from across the political spectrum that reflect how complex issues attract many shades of opinion.*

A **global** *emphasis with foreign perspectives and surveys on various moral questions and political issues that will help readers to place subject matter in a less culture-bound and ethnocentric frame of reference. In an ever-shrinking and interdependent world, understanding and cooperation are essential. Many issues are global in nature and can be effectively dealt with only by common efforts and international understanding.*

Reasoning skill *study guides and discussion activities provide ready-made tools for helping with critical reading and evaluation of content. The guides and activities deal with one or more of the following:*

RECOGNIZING AUTHOR'S POINT OF VIEW

INTERPRETING EDITORIAL CARTOONS

VALUES IN CONFLICT

WHAT IS EDITORIAL BIAS?

WHAT IS SEX BIAS?

WHAT IS POLITICAL BIAS?

WHAT IS ETHNOCENTRIC BIAS?

WHAT IS RACE BIAS?

WHAT IS RELIGIOUS BIAS?

*From across **the political spectrum** varied sources are presented for research projects and classroom discussions. Diverse opinions in the series come from magazines, newspapers, syndicated columnists, books, political speeches, foreign nations, and position papers by corporations and nonprofit institutions.*

About the Editor

Gary E. McCuen is an editor and publisher of anthologies for public libraries and curriculum materials for schools. Over the past years his publications have specialized in social, moral and political conflict. They include books, pamphlets, cassettes, tabloids, filmstrips and simulation games, many of them designed from his curriculums during 11 years of teaching junior and senior high school social studies. At present he is the editor and publisher of the *Ideas in Conflict* series and the *Editorial Forum* series.

CHAPTER 1

EUTHANASIA:
INTRODUCTION AND OVERVIEW

1   EUTHANASIA:
INTRODUCTION AND OVERVIEW

PHYSICIAN-ASSISTED SUICIDE &
PHYSICIAN AID-IN-DYING:
AN OVERVIEW

Christopher Grant Docker

The following excerpt was taken from an article published by Christopher Grant Docker. He is the Executive Secretary of the Voluntary Euthanasia Society of Scotland.

Points to Consider:

1. Compare / contrast physician-assisted suicide with physician aid-in-dying.

2. What advantages for the patient are inherent in physician aid-in-dying?

3. What advantages for the physician are inherent in physician-assisted suicide?

Christopher Grant Docker, "Physician-Assisted Suicide and Physician Aid-in-Dying," Voluntary Euthanasia Society of Scotland, 1993.

Killing oneself painlessly and in a dignified manner that will not cause unnecessary suffering to oneself or others is a difficult business.

Physician-assisted suicide is the provision by a doctor, consciously and legally, to a patient who has competently requested it, of the means for that patient to end his or her own life. The "means" usually implies lethal drugs that can cause death painlessly, such as a large quantity of barbiturates, or else apparatus comprising carbon monoxide and inhaling mask, as provided by Dr. Kevorkian of Michigan, U.S.A.

The phrase "physician-assisted suicide" is widely accepted parlance in the U.S.A. Etymologists will note, in passing, that the word "physician" does not semantically imply the paternalism inherent in the word "doctor" – which combines the superiority of the "teacher" with the "docility" of the disciple...

Suicide is a non-criminal act, yet the law currently in Britain makes it illegal to assist, or even supply the means, for a competent adult to engage in this non-criminal act.

THE ROLE OF DOCTORS

In cases of unbearable and unrelievable suffering or indignity, physician-assisted suicide leaves no doubt as to the fact that the patient made the final decision. Doctors who commit suicide, statistically, are able to use sure and painless drugs. Those methods are not available to other members of society, and a doctor who makes them available is liable to criminal charges. Methods used by people who are not able to obtain such drugs need careful planning and preparation to avoid added suffering, pain and indignity. Killing oneself is easy (though not that easy); killing oneself painlessly and in a dignified manner that will not cause unnecessary suffering to oneself or others is a difficult business.

Laws are less severe in other European countries although medical paternalism or social disapproval can still negate much of the law's rationale. The advantages of a physician prescribing drugs also include the prospect of dialogue, so that the patient can more fully examine and exhaust other options with the physician. The very prospect would mean a closer bond with the doctor – one less "taboo". One would know that if illness got so bad that life no longer held out any promise of meaningful existence, one could still turn to the doctor for support and respect, rather than

Illustration by Craig MacIntosh. Reprinted with permission from the **Star Tribune**, Minneapolis.

the loneliness and pain of a bottle of paracetamol.

Doctors I have spoken to are, by and large, remarkably uninformed about drugs that reliably can be taken orally to induce death. They know that many drugs might well cause death, that certain dosages are toxic, but they have received no training and have little or no knowledge of what amounts will reliably cause death. The "reliability" factor is the all-important one to the patient who wants to be 100% sure of the result. Prescribing drugs is far less traumatic a prospect for some doctors than giving a lethal injection (physician aid-in-dying) and has the moral safeguard already mentioned of ensuring that the patient has the final control. It is seen by a number of legal draftsmen in America as a more logical "next step" than seeking immediate legislation on physician-assisted suicide. Legislation could be permissive in nature, so that a doctor with a conscientious objection to discussing such a request in an unbiased fashion and subsequently perhaps prescribing the drugs, could refer a patient to another doctor, as happens with abortion. The ability to "leave by the door marked EXIT" should the final need arise, gives many patients the courage to go on much longer. This has been demonstrated in many cases, and is also well known in Netherlands (where the same sense of reassurance is conveyed by an approval of an application for physician aid-in-dying, so that the patient knows that such aid will definitely be available if his or her request continues).

PHYSICIAN AID-IN-DYING

Physician aid-in-dying is assistance by a qualified medical practitioner in implementing a patient's considered wish to end his or her own life, usually by means of lethal injection. In the Netherlands, the practice is an injection to render the patient comatose, followed by a second injection to stop the heart. In

PHYSICIAN AID-IN-DYING

Physician Aid-in-Dying is assistance by a qualified medical practitioner in implementing a patient's considered wish to end his or her own life, usually by means of lethal injection.

The Voluntary Euthanasia Society of Scotland, May 5, 1993

cases where the patient takes the lethal drug, currently 10g of pentobarbitone, the doctor is present; in the 20% of cases where death does not occur within twelve hours, the doctor is on hand to administer a second drug to accelerate death, rather than allow the patient the indignity of lying in a coma for up to four days for death to occur.

Objections that the legalization of the practice would be open to abuse are not sustained by close examination of data. Patients are already "eased into death" with morphine under the euphemistic doctrine of "double effect". Published figures suggest that ethical criteria in the Netherlands are similar to those already practiced in this country. Legal safeguards for the various situations have been thoroughly prepared by legal researchers in draft legislation. Trends show that the practice will continue whether or not it is regulated by legislation.

Although the possibility of physician-assisted suicide is welcome news to many people who may be facing the prospect of an agonizing, humiliating and long drawn-out disease while still having some physical capabilities, it is of little reassurance to someone who is suffering from a wasting disease that will eventually rob him of the physical ability to commit suicide. Also, death by oral ingestion of drugs is far less sure than by skillful injection. A doctor on hand can make necessary adjustments of dosage for the patient's weight, condition, age, and history, and also take the necessary action if something goes wrong. This, in essence, is the Dutch argument, and although drugs are often made available for the patient to take orally by his or her own hand, if and when desired and after due consultation, a physician is generally present to offer the technical support that a patient has the right to expect.

2

EUTHANASIA:
INTRODUCTION AND OVERVIEW

HISTORICAL PERSPECTIVES:
PHYSICIAN AID-IN-DYING
(Active Voluntary Euthanasia)

Edwin R. Dubose

Edwin R. DuBose wrote the following article in his capacity as contributing editor at The Park Ridge Center. The article presents historical perspectives on euthanasia. It was published by the Park Ridge Center in Chicago, 676 North St. Clair, Suite 450, Chicago, Illinois 60611.

Points to Consider:

1. Explain the Greek concept of a "good death" and "freedom to leave".

2. What early Christian beliefs about human life and suffering prohibited euthanasia?

3. How did nineteenth century medical advances bring in the age of "heroic medicine"?

4. Contrast "passive euthanasia" with "active euthanasia".

Edwin R. DuBose, "A Brief Historical Perspective on Euthanasia," excerpted from a book by the Park Ridge Center and now distributed by Trinity Press International, P.O. Box 851 Valley Forge, PA 19482. Ron Hamel, Edwin R. Dubose and Martin E. Marty, **Active Euthanasia, Religion and the Public Debate** (Chicago, Illinois: The Park Ridge Center, 1991). pp. 17-24. Reprinted with permission.

For the Romans and the Greeks, dying decently and rationally mattered immensely.

Active voluntary euthanasia is not new to the latter part of the twentieth century. Even in ancient societies, terminally ill people requested to have their dying hastened, though the meaning of euthanasia for them differed from its meaning today. What seems new is the cultural context in which the question of euthanasia arises. Many factors contribute to this new context, but perhaps most influential are the sophistication and availability of medical technology and the social, scientific, moral, and religious beliefs that permeate modern American society...

Because the English word euthanasia is taken from the Greek *eu thanatos*, "good or easy death", this review begins with classical antiquity.

CLASSICAL ANTIQUITY

In the present day the term euthanasia is associated with the act of mercifully ending the life of a hopelessly suffering patient. The classical understanding of what is now called euthanasia, however, was broader in scope. Focusing on the act of hastening death, the contemporary question involving euthanasia tends to be: Is euthanasia under any conditions morally justifiable? For the ancients, in contrast, euthanasia did not necessarily imply an act, a means, or a method of causing or hastening death. The focus was on one possible manner of dying, and the pivotal question was; Did the person voluntarily meet death with peace of mind and minimal pain? The Greeks sometimes employed the term to describe the "spiritual" state of the dying person at the impending moment of death; it was important that the person die a "good death", in a psychologically balanced state of mind, under composed circumstances, in a condition of self-control. To ensure such a death, it was permissible to shorten a person's life.

Moreover, for the Greeks and Romans, a "good death" was not anchored in a medical context alone, nor did it carry the contemporary negative connotations of suicide. Their stress was on the voluntary and reasoned nature of the dying, and they were generally sympathetic to active voluntary euthanasia, provided that the deed was done for the right reasons, for example, to end the suffering of a terminal illness. In this sense, the English language has lost touch with many of the characteristic Greek and Roman

15

understandings of active euthanasia, which tended to emphasize it as a mode of death, a way of dying, carefully distinguished from murder or suicide.

In classical antiquity, then, there was a generally recognized, although qualified, tolerance of the "freedom to leave", which permitted the sick or suffering to terminate their lives. Furthermore, under the appropriate circumstances, it was permissible for others to administer the means of death...

THE CHRISTIAN ERA

For the Romans and the Greeks, dying decently and rationally mattered immensely. In a sense, how they died was a measure of the final value of life, especially for a life wasted by disease and suffering. For early Christians, however, this was not a consideration. Because only God had the right to give and take life, active euthanasia was viewed as an illicit exercise of a divine prerogative.

Generally, the practice of active euthanasia among the sick became unusual after about the second century A.D., because of the growing acceptance of the importance placed by Judeo-Christian teachings upon individual life and the endurance of suffering. By the fifth century, Augustine held that life and its suffering were divinely ordained by God and must be borne accordingly. A human was created in the image of God, and his or her life thus belonged to God; the time and manner of death was God's will and God's only. Moreover, as the writings of the New Testament assumed canonical form, suffering was viewed by Christians as something in which they could rejoice for two reasons: (1) God used suffering as a means of producing spiritual maturity; and (2) the very fact that Christians endured suffering was proof that they were children of God. Christians were to engage in an active, direct ministry of consolation and encouragement of their fellow sufferers. The relief to be provided was not removal of the suffering but a consolation that transformed the suffering into a positive force in the person's life. Thus the belief developed that one should not abandon the life assigned to him or her by God but should endure it in the hope of a certain resurrection. These influences helped to shape social, moral, and religious attitudes toward illness and disability and acceptance of suffering at the time of death. As the ethic of respect for human life achieved this moral status, the early Christians declared it the

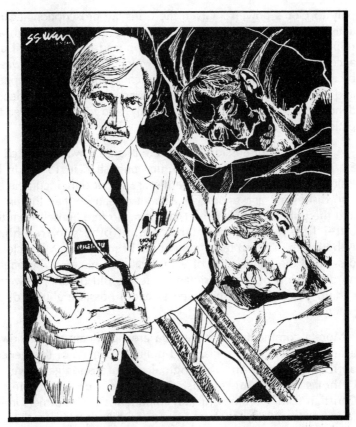

Cartoon by David Seavey. Copyright 1984, **USA Today**. Reprinted with permission.

absolute standard of right conduct for doctor and patient alike. Finally, although Christian charity brought a heightened sense of responsibility to relieve suffering, the Biblical commandment against killing seemed to prohibit absolutely the taking of a person's life even to relieve suffering.

During the next eight centuries, views of euthanasia were shaped by moral and legal prohibitions endorsed by the authority of the Catholic church. In the thirteenth century, Thomas Aquinas argued that shortening one's life was sinful not only because it violated a commandment but because it left no time for the person's repentance. Also, taking one's own life or the life of another was against the law of nature and contrary to charity. Such an act was not lawful because every person belonged to the community, and it was a sin against God because life was a gift and subject only to God's powers. Given the Christian proscriptions against active euthanasia for any reason, the sense of a "good" death was reinterpreted: the Christian was supposed to be tranquil and accepting at death. The means by which this acceptance was to be achieved included primarily physical comfort, moral support, and prayer. This essentially passive process was largely independent of the physician; the clergy, family, and friends prepared the patient for a good, "Christian" death.

A theoretical discussion of active euthanasia was presented by Sir Thomas More in his *Utopia*, first published in 1516. In his vision of the ideal society, "if a disease is not only incurable but also distressing and agonizing without cessation, then the priests and the public officials exhort the man...to free himself from this bitter life...or else voluntarily permit others to free him." Although the English term had not yet been coined, More clearly described the active form of euthanasia. In his essay he offered no discussion of the physician's role; he did outline, however, certain precautions to be taken to avoid possible abuses of the practice.

More's comments on euthanasia are significant when viewed against the religious, social, and political climate of this general period. As gathering theological storm clouds gave way to Luther's thundering against Rome, one's understanding of Christian faith became crucially important. The reformers in the reign of Henry VIII, to whom More succumbed, and later those in Elizabeth's reign, faced a formidable task in converting the people to Protestantism. Following an Augustinian argument against euthanasia as an evil caused by a lack of faith, they viewed euthanasia as the antithesis of the faith that every Christian needed in order to be saved; it represented the opposite of pious hope...

THE NINETEENTH CENTURY

The role of the physician in dealing with the dying patient received significant attention in the early nineteenth century. During the previous decades, the enthusiasms of the Enlightenment faith in human progress led to the elaboration of a number of ambitious, this-worldly alternatives to Christian attitudes toward illness, suffering and death. Because of the human ability to know and control the natural, physical world, a number of Enlightenment philosophers believed that biomedical research, public health programs, and progressive thinking would result in a

18

much extended life span. Now that science had been freed from religion's superstition and ignorance, Benjamin Franklin predicted, the new scientific and medical advances would make possible human longevity of a thousand years or more. In spite of this optimism, however, by 1800 the limits of medical achievement were recognized. Medicine, it was argued, could not conquer death, but the physician could marshal medicine's forces to slow down the tragically inevitable process of decline. As part of the effort to ward off premature death, new devices were developed to prevent pain and relieve distress, and these required the expert intervention and guidance of the medical profession and inaugurated the age of heroic medicine.

This new level of medical intervention to prolong life prompted the criticism that physicians were needlessly prolonging the dying process. A number of articles written in Europe and America during the late eighteenth and early nineteenth centuries criticized physicians who treated diseases rather than patients. Many of these pieces discussed the role of the physician in promoting the classical notion of harmonious death. After noting the tendency of physicians to neglect a patient once an illness was found to be terminal, the author of one article in 1826 urged doctors to accept responsibility for their patients' "spiritual" euthanasia. Physical and moral comfort were to be provided, but heroic medications likely to prolong the dying and extend a person's suffering were to be avoided. At the same time, the author condemned the thought of hastening a patient's death. However, medical and therapeutic advances during the century made heroic intervention increasingly possible and set the stage for open advocacy of the practice of active euthanasia...

Samuel D. Williams, schoolmaster and essayist, in 1870 published the first paper to deal entirely with the concept of active voluntary euthanasia and its application. There he advocated active euthanasia for all willing patients with incurable and painful diseases. Williams further argued that it was the duty of medical attendants, presumably physicians, to provide active euthanasia to their patients. Neither concern that pain and suffering should be nobly borne until a natural death nor the sense that one's life belonged to God entered his argument.

By the beginning of the twentieth century, the major elements in the contemporary arguments for and against the practice of active voluntary euthanasia had been articulated. The growth of scientific knowledge and technology led to a reconsideration of traditional moral views, accompanied by a decline in the importance of theology in shaping social views of suicide and euthanasia. Some physicians admitted having practiced active euthanasia, and others expressed sympathy for the practice. Other physicians, however, found no medical precedent to justify the sacrifice of life and believed that the practice would lead to abuses, and, being illegal, would be regarded as murder. Many others continued to see life as God's gift, not to be taken lightly or curtailed prematurely. Thus many people believed that the issue could not be settled in light of moral and religious concerns, and more attention was given to its legal aspects. As a compromise, some people began to advocate what they called "passive euthanasia". At that time, the term referred to the avoidance of extreme or heroic measures to prolong life in cases of incurable and painful illness; advocates maintained that treatment should be withheld not to hasten death but to avoid the pain and suffering of prolonged dying. This development paved the way for more contemporary controversies surrounding the issue of withdrawing medical treatment, which today is associated with the term passive euthanasia.

The line between active killing for mercy and withdrawing or withholding medical treatment has been, until recently, a critical part of an ethic for the care of the terminally or critically ill. With recent cases in which decisions to withdraw medically supplied nutrition and hydration are legally sanctioned, people are raising questions about the validity of the sharp moral and legal distinction between passive and active euthanasia.

INTERPRETING EDITORIAL CARTOONS

This activity may be used as an individualized study guide for students in libraries and resource centers or as a discussion catalyst in small group and classroom discussions.

Although cartoons are usually humorous, the main intent of most political cartoonists is not to entertain. Cartoons express serious social comment about important issues. Using graphic and visual arts, the cartoonist expresses opinions and attitudes. By employing an entertaining and often light-hearted visual format, cartoonists may have as much or more impact on national and world issues as editorial and syndicated columnists.

Points to Consider:

1. Examine the cartoon on page 17.

2. How would you describe the message of the cartoon? Try to describe the message in one to three sentences.

3. Do you agree with the message expressed in the cartoon? Why or why not?

4. Does the cartoon support the author's point of view in any of the readings in this publication? If the answer is yes, be specific about which reading or readings and why.

5. Is either of the readings in Chapter One in basic agreement with the cartoon?

CHAPTER 2

DR. KEVORKIAN AND ASSISTED SUICIDE

3   DR. KEVORKIAN AND ASSISTED SUICIDE

THE KEVORKIAN CHRONICLES: Three Years of Assisted Suicides – An Overview

Detroit News

The following time-line appeared in the Detroit News.

Points to Consider:

1. Summarize the nature of the diseases of the various suicide cases.

2. What legal measures were taken by the State of Michigan?

3. What is Kevorkian's rationale for his role in the suicides?

"The Kevorkian Chronicles: Three Years of Assisted Suicide," **Detroit News**, May 17, 1993. Reprinted with permission.

June 5, 1990: Janet Adkins, a 54-year-old Portland, Ore., woman suffering from Alzheimer's disease, takes her life by using a suicide machine developed by Kevorkian.

June 8, 1990: Oakland County Circuit Judge Alice Gilbert temporarily bars Kevorkian from using his machine to help others commit suicide.

December 13, 1990: A murder charge against Kevorkian in the Adkins case is dropped when Rochester Hills District Judge Gerald McNally rules Michigan has no law prohibiting assisted suicide.

February 5, 1991: Gilbert makes her injunction against Kevorkian permanent, blocking him from using his machine to help people commit suicide. Gilbert writes that Kevorkian's "real goal is self-service, not patient service" and that he exhibited "bizarre" behavior that disgraced the medical profession.

October 23, 1991: Kevorkian helps Sherry Miller, 43, of Roseville and Marjorie Wantz, 58, of Sodus, Mich., take their lives. Miller had multiple sclerosis and Wantz had severe pelvic pain. Miller uses a machine similar to one used by Adkdins. Wantz inhales carbon monoxide.

November 20, 1991: The Michigan Board of Medicine suspends Kevorkian's license to practice.

February, 1992: Kevorkian is ordered to stand trial on murder charges in the deaths of Miller and Wantz.

May 15, 1992: Susan Williams, 52, of Clawson, dies by carbon monoxide poisoning. Kevorkian and his attorney claim Kevorkian advised but did not assist in the suicide. Williams had multiple sclerosis. That death has been ruled a homicide but Kevorkian has not been charged.

July 21, 1992: Oakland County Circuit Judge David Breck dismisses murder charges against Kevorkian in the deaths of Miller and Wantz. He echoes McNally in saying Michigan has no law against assisted suicide.

September 26, 1992: Lois F. Hawes, 52, of Warren, dies after placing a mask over her face and turning on a canister of carbon monoxide. She had terminal lung cancer.

November 23, 1992: Catherine A. Andreyev, 45, of Moon

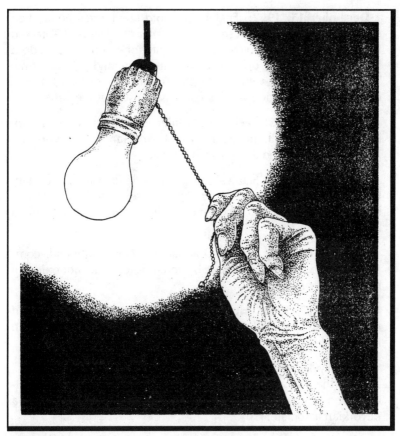

Illustration by Craig MacIntosh. Reprinted with permission from the **Star Tribune**, Minneapolis.

Township, Pa., dies in Kevorkian's presence by inhaling carbon monoxide gas. She had terminal cancer.

November 24, 1992: The Michigan House approves legislation temporarily banning assisted suicide in Michigan.

December 3, 1992: The State Senate approves the assisted suicide ban, sending the measure to Gov. John Engler for his signature.

December 15, 1992: Marguerite Tate, 70, of Auburn Hills and Marcella Lawrence, 67, of Clinton Township become the seventh and eighth women to die with Kevorkian's help. Both die by inhaling carbon monoxide.

December 15, 1992: Engler signs into law the temporary ban on assisted suicide, about seven hours after the deaths of Tate and Lawrence. The law makes helping someone commit suicide a felony punishable by up to four years in prison and a $2,000 fine. The legislation takes effect March 30 and imposes a 15-month ban on assisted suicide while a commission studies the issue.

January 20, 1993: Jack Elmer Miller, 53, of Huron Township, becomes the first man to die with Kevorkian's help when he inhales carbon monoxide through a mask.

February 4, 1993: Stanley Ball, 82, of Leland, Mich., and Mary Biernat, 73, of Crown Point, Ind., kill themselves in Ball's lakeside bungalow by inhaling carbon monoxide gas from tanks supplied by Kevorkian.

February 8, 1993: Elaine Goldbaum, 47, of Southfield, commits suicide in her apartment by inhaling carbon monoxide in Kevorkian's presence.

February 15, 1993: Hugh Gale, 70, of Roseville, who suffered from emphysema and congestive heart disease, kills himself in Kevorkian's presence by inhaling carbon monoxide.

February 18, 1993: Jonathon Grenz, 44, of Costa Mesa, Calif., and Martha Ruwart, 41, of Cardiff-by the-Sea, Calif., die by inhaling carbon monoxide. The two died at the Waterford home of a Kevorkian associate.

February 25, 1993: Spurred on by the three assisted suicides the week before, the Michigan Legislature approves a bill that makes the assisted suicide ban effective immediately. The ban goes into effect shortly after Engler signs the bill at 5 p.m.

February 25, 1993: Oakland and Macomb prosecutors obtain a search warrant, based on a document a right-to-life advocate told them she found in the garbage of a longtime Kevorkian associate, Neal Nicol. Macomb County Prosecutor Carl Marlinga and Oakland County Prosecutor Richard Thompson allege the minutes of the death of Hugh Gale were altered to hide the fact Gale twice asked that the mask be taken off his face. The prosecutors say the case is being investigated as a homicide.

April 27, 1993: Macomb County prosecutors exonerate Kevorkian in Gale's death, saying testimony from witnesses corroborate Kevorkian's assertion Gale wanted to kill himself.

KEVORKIAN ATTENDS 19TH SUICIDE

Dr. Jack Kevorkian was at the scene of a 19th suicide Friday, this time at his apartment.

The retired pathologist was present when Merian Frederick, a 72-year-old woman with Lou Gehrig's disease, killed herself by inhaling carbon monoxide.

Kevorkian, 65, maintains that the terminally ill have the right to commit suicide with a doctor's help. He already faces two charges of assisting suicide in violation of a Michigan law passed specifically to stop him.

"Kevorkian Attends 19th Suicide," **Associated Press**, October, 1993

April 27, 1993: A California administrative law judge, acting on a request from the state medical board, suspends Kevorkian's medical license. Kevorkian has the right to a hearing within 30 days to determine if his license, granted in 1957, should be revoked.

May 16, 1993: Kevorkian attends the suicide of Ronald Mansur, 54, of Southfield, the first such suicide since the practice was outlawed in Michigan.

(**Editor's Note:** Dr. Jack Kevorkian has been charged by the State of Michigan in two cases with illegally assisting a suicide. Kevorkian and the American Civil Liberties Union have challenged the Michigan law that makes assisted suicide illegal. A Michigan judge released Kevorkian from jail after he promised not to assist in any suicides until all legal issues surrounding the cases between Kevorkian and the State of Michigan have been resolved. Dr. Kevorkian has begun a petition drive to legalize assisted suicide in Michigan. He has assisted in the suicide of 20 people.)

4 DR. KEVORKIAN AND ASSISTED SUICIDE

MEDICIDE: THE GOODNESS OF PLANNED DEATH

Dr. Jack Kevorkian

Jack Kevorkian, M.D. has gained international media attention within the past several years for his work in assisting terminally ill patients to end their lives.

Points to Consider:

1. What does Dr. Kevorkian view as the highest principle in medical ethics?

2. Identify the two patient components and three doctor components in a planned death.

3. Summarize the positive benefits of planned death according to Kevorkian.

4. Analyze: "Assisted suicide is a higher ethical act of self-determination than euthanasia."

Paul Kurtz interviews Dr. Jack Kevorkian, "Medicide: The Goodness of Planned Death," **Free Inquiry**, Fall 1991. Reprinted with permission.

We call it the "mercitron".

Free Inquiry: Dr. Kevorkian, you've been involved in a number of battles, particularly in the last year, that have received public attention. What is your main interest? What are you trying to get across to the public?

Jack Kevorkian: I suppose my main interest is to reinstitute an ethical medical practice, which today is more necessary and more needed than ever, to extract from inevitable human death benefit in the form of life-prolonging maneuvers.

FI: Can you amplify what you mean by "extract benefit from death"?

JK: Death under any circumstances is negative – it's a loss of human life. Today we have death that's mandated: There are prisoners and there are terminally ill, crippled, or incapacitated people who, for various reasons, kill themselves. To some degree these may be beneficial acts for the individuals, perhaps to their families, or to society in the case of prisoners. But still, all the benefits put together cannot counterbalance the negativity of the loss of a human life.

FI: Is life cherished in itself?

JK: Yes. This is not a matter of divinity or sanctity, but of empirical existence.

FI: Life is good.

JK: That's beyond argument! Whether any specific individual's life is good or bad is a matter of judgment; but life itself is a prerequisite for existence, for a meaningful existence.

FI: Life becomes a value.

JK: Yes, it's the highest value because everything else depends on life.

FI: What position do you take regarding terminal patients who are dying?

JK: In my view the highest principle in medical ethics – in any kind of ethics – is personal autonomy, self-determination. What counts is what the patient wants and judges to be a benefit or a value in his or her own life. That's primary.

Now, if a patient is suffering from some kind of debilitating condition and says, "I want to end my life. It's no longer worth going on," value is diminishing. The patient should go to a medical person, as this is primarily a medical problem. If the patient wishes he can go to a theologian or a sociologist, but that won't solve the medical problem. It's the medical problem that's causing this shift in values in the patient's own mind, so the patient goes to a doctor.

Now, let's assume the doctor personifies the medical field. The doctor would then have to judge whether the patient's wishes are medically justified. I break this down into five components, of which the patient has two and the doctor three. The patient's components are wish and need: The wish to terminate his or her life, which stems from a need felt because of the suffering.

FI: *Does this have to be a reflective or a rational choice?*

JK: It should be, it must be, rational. Emotions certainly play a part. Emotions color life. But emotions cannot be the major basis for a decision. Humanity is characterized by one faculty which so-called lower animals don't have — reason. Reason must predominate.

FI: *You're talking here about competent adults, of course?*

JK: Yes.

FI: *What are the three components for the doctor?*

JK: The doctor has three tools. One is basic common sense, which is difficult to define, but I think we all know what it is.

FI: *Common sense is a kind of reflective, sensible analysis of the patient's situation.*

JK: Almost all of humanity would agree on that. For example, if the stove is red hot, don't touch it. Now, a Hindu guru might think differently, touch it, and say it's not hot. But most of humanity would agree that common sense says not to touch the stove.

The second tool that we are supposed to prize so highly is rationality. Ratiocination is actually a better word. That would be defined as "clear thinking".

Illustration by Darren Brettingen.

The third tool is the most important – medical expertise. That's why the patient would go to a doctor instead of a theologian. Almost all doctors have the medical expertise. Unfortunately, fewer have common sense and rationality, and this is a problem.

If the doctor has common sense and uses ratiocination and his medical expertise, he can evaluate every nuance of the medical problem and decide whether the patient's desire to end his or her life is justified. No other professional can do this, and that's what takes this out of the realm of bioethics as espoused by nonphysicians who are medically ignorant and, therefore, ignorant of the foundation of this whole system.

FI: *So in your system the patient makes the choice. The doctor merely analyzes the situation and provides the means for the patient to terminate his or her life.*

JK: Yes. As an analogy, let's say a patient goes to a doctor-surgeon and says, "Doctor, I want my appendix out." The patient has a desire. The doctor can't affect the desire, but he can determine the need. So the surgeon would say, "Oh really?" and then do a history, a physical, and laboratory tests to determine whether there is a valid need.

31

FI: *The title of your new book is* Prescription: Medicide — The Goodness of Planned Death. *What does "planned death" involve?*

JK: Planned death is a rational system that honors self-determination and extracts from a purposeful, unavoidable death the maximum benefit for the subject, the subject's next of kin, and for all of humanity. In other words, planned death is a system for making death, euthanasia, and suicide positive instead of negative.

FI: *And one positive benefit is that the patient will not suffer agonizing pain and torment.*

JK: That's a minor benefit. That the family will suffer less psychological pain and loss of assets is also minor, as well as that society will be spared the waste of some resources. Three minor benefits do not counter-balance the loss of a human life. But if the patient opts for euthanasia, or if someone is to be executed, and at the same time opts to donate organs, he or she can save anywhere from five to ten lives. Now the death becomes definitely, incalculably positive. The patient may opt to undergo experimentation under anesthesia, from which he or she won't awaken. This could affect millions of lives now and in the future. If the person wants only to donate organs, that's fine. The ultimate value is autonomy.

So the patient would have several choices, which don't exist now, besides just wanting to be put to death. The patient can say, "Fine, I just want to be put to death." That's option one. Or the patient can say: "I want to have organs taken out under anesthesia from which I won't awaken." That's option two. Or the patient can say, "You can experiment on me, under anesthesia from which I won't awaken." That's option three. And there are yet more options under number three such as the option to choose the experiment.

FI: *What kinds of experiments are you talking about?*

JK: Any kind. Whatever the patient wants. For example, if the patient is dying of Lou Gehrig's disease, he can stipulate that the experiment must deal with that affliction. The doctor and the researchers would be bound by that wish. Another sub-option would be to allow the doctor to do any experiment he or she wants.

FI: *Wouldn't there be fear that the patient would suffer pain and torment if experimentation is allowed on his body while he or she is still alive?*

JK: Well, the patient would be under anesthesia. Anyone who's had a major operation knows that the patient would be unaware of any pain or discomfort.

FI: *What guarantee would the patient have that he or she would not suffer in this situation?*

JK: The patient would be under constantly controlled anesthesia. The procedure would not be done privately or secretly. There would be witnesses: the patient's attorney, or the patient's family members if they wish to be there, the patient's minister or priest or rabbi, and one or two other authorities...

FI: *Let us focus on euthanasia. There is passive euthanasia, in which people are not kept alive by the use of extraordinary methods, and ...*

JK: That's not euthanasia. "Passive euthanasia" is a misnomer. "Passive euthanasia" is just natural death. Euthanasia means "good death". "Passive euthanasia" is a brutal death. Allowing someone to starve to death and to die of thirst, the way we do now, is barbaric. Our Supreme Court has validated barbarism. The Nazis did that in the concentration camps.

FI: *So, not leaving the respirator on, pulling the plug — that's not a good death?*

JK: Gasping for air? Starving and thirsting to death? Like Nancy Cruzan: it took her a week to die. Try it! You think that just because you're in a coma you don't suffer?

FI: Let's go on to active euthanasia.

JK: Drop the word active. Euthanasia by definition has to be active, otherwise it's assisted suicide.

FI: Let's take the case of giving increasing dosages of morphine.

JK: That's euthanasia. When the doctor gives the pills or "shots", he or she's the agent of death.

FI: So euthanasia is the hastening of the process of death.

JK: That's right — but mercifully.

FI: Now, you go beyond that. You advocate assisted suicide and have constructed a "suicide machine".

JK: We call it the "mercitron".

FI: What's the difference between the mercitron and active euthanasia?

JK: It's like giving someone a loaded gun. The patient pulls the trigger, not the doctor. If the doctor sets up the needle and syringe but lets the patient push the plunger, that's assisted suicide. If the doctor pushed the plunger it would be euthanasia.

FI: In your view assisted suicide is a higher ethical act of self-determination than euthanasia?

JK: Yes. It's more ethical and less vulnerable to censure because the patient himself is more directly involved. The only one actually committing the act is the patient. That's why assisted suicide, where possible, is always preferable to euthanasia. That's the way executions should be carried out, an idea that has been suggested by four condemned prisoners I've had contact with.

FI: What do you mean by the term "medicide"?

JK: Medicide is euthanasia performed by a professional medical person — a doctor, nurse, technician, paramedic, or nurse anesthetist, for example. Euthanasia is humane, merciful death, performed by anybody. When the patient allows organ transplants or experimentation, it's called "obitiatry". Obitiatry is medicide from which the actual medical benefit is extracted for other human beings.

34

5 DR. KEVORKIAN AND ASSISTED SUICIDE

SUICIDE DOCTOR SHOULD BE PROSECUTED

Arthur Caplan

Arthur Caplan is the director of the Center for Biomedical Ethics at the University of Pennsylvania. He also directed the Center for Biomedical Ethics at the University of Minnesota.

Points to Consider:

1. Summarize the response of the medical community to the death of Adkins.

2. What is Caplan's objection to Kevorkian being a pathologist?

3. Comment on: "Alzheimers…characterized by the loss of insight and judgment" as related to Adkins' death.

4. Analyze: "…we are so blinded by our fears of disability, dying and death."

Arthur Caplan, "Suicide Machine Merits Prosecution, Not Praise," **The Baltimore Sun**, June 19, 1990. Reprinted with permission.

Why can't we see that what Kevorkian did with Janet Adkins merits not praise but prosecution?

Sometime June 4, Dr. Jack Kevorkian, a retired pathologist and self-promoting, self-styled free-thinker, drove a 54-year-old Portland, Oregon, woman, Janet Adkins, in his old VW van out to a trailer park on the outskirts of Detroit. He says he attached her arm to his homemade euthanasia machine and monitored her heartbeat while she used it to kill herself. Kevorkian says he hopes Janet Adkins' death will force the issue of euthanasia into the public spotlight. Incredibly, it is doing that.

MEDIA COVERAGE

The reaction to Kevorkian's bizarre actions has been swift and lamentable. The media instantly anointed him a celebrity. Eager to succeed in a role he has long sought, Kevorkian is now in the midst of a whirlwind tour of the TV talk shows. There he blathers on about the need to create, in his charming terminology, "obitoriums" — places where people can use his suicide machine in a setting that has more ambiance than a trailer park. The obitoriums, Kevorkian declaims to a seemingly unending parade of stylishly coiffed heads and flawless teeth, will be administered by "untouchables" — people of impeccable moral character who will operate the facilities in a not-for-profit manner.

The legal authorities in Michigan reacted to Kevorkian's drive in the park as if their brains had been attached to his lethal contraption. While a judge did issue an order prohibiting the good doctor from killing anyone else in the confines of Oakland County, the medical examiner and the district attorney avowed that it would take them anywhere from two weeks to two months to figure out what to do with Kevorkian. Tests must be performed on Adkins' body to establish cause of death. Apparently, Kevorkian's unending series of televised boasts are circumventing Detroit.

THE MEDICAL COMMUNITY

The medical community seems to believe that mumbling is the appropriate response when a doctor claims he took someone he barely knew into a park to help her die. Many doctors hinted that euthanasia is a fact of medical life. Others said at least he had drawn attention to an important issue of public policy. Several murmured that he had pushed into uncharted legal territory.

36

"AND NOW I'LL DEMONSTRATE MY LITTLE MACHINE IF WE COULD HAVE A VOLUNTEER WHO'S NOT FEELING UP TO PAR TODAY!"

Cartoon by Wayne Stayskal. Reprinted by permission: Tribune Media Services.

It is more accurate to say that Kevorkian's excursion took him right through uncharted legal territory into an ethical Twilight Zone. Is this suicide a reasonable foundation for a discussion of the ethics of euthanasia?

Kevorkian helped kill someone whom he says he met for the first time two days earlier. After explaining his machine to Adkins over dinner, he apparently decided she was competent to make the choice to kill herself.

This is, to be polite, a moral outrage. Kevorkian is a pathologist, not a psychologist or psychiatrist. He has limited experience in dealing with living patients. His stock in trade was examining dead ones. Could he really be confident that Janet Adkins wanted to die based upon two days of personal contact and one dinner conversation? Did the fact that her husband bought her a round-trip ticket give him pause?

Janet Adkins decided to kill herself when she learned that she had Alzheimer's disease. Let's assume the diagnosis was correct. Would the fact that she had Alzheimer's complicate the assessment of her competence to decide to kill herself?

A KILLING MACHINE

Had Kevorkian made a noose for Janet Adkins to hang her-self with, or helped her point a gun at her head and indicated when to pull the trigger, there seems little doubt that he would have been charged with and convicted of manslaughter (the reckless endangerment of another's life), if not murder. Had he simply prescribed medication for her, and informed her that taking a certain number of pills was likely to cause death, it is unlikely he would have been charged with anything. But he took an intermediate position: devising his own machine which has no medical use, but because of the IV and drugs involved, seems to be a medical machine. The suicide machine stands as a hybrid between medical and nonmedical technology. Judge McNally ultimately saw this machine as medical in nature, and the act of using it one that a physician performs for a patient. That is why Kevorkian was treated much more kindly than the man who later came to Michigan to help his wife commit suicide, and was charged with murder for, among other things, tying a plastic bag over her head.

George J. Annas, "Killing Machines," **Hastings Center Report**, March-April, 1991

ALZHEIMER'S PATIENTS

Mario Mendez is a physician who is a behavioral neurologist specializing in the treatment of Alzheimer's patients at St. Paul-Ramsey Medical Center. He says that what is most troubling about Alzheimer's is that "it is an especially insidious disease...characterized by the loss of insight and judgment" about one's own decisions and behavior. Did Janet Adkins really know what she was doing when she told Kevorkian to hitch her up to his death device?

Kevorkian is disqualified from even trying to answer this question. He has spent the past few years promoting his ideas about the desirability of euthanasia, obitoriums, killing prisoners in a way that permits the salvage of their organs for transplantation and marketing his goofy, homemade death machine. Putting aside the huge boulder of conflict of interest, was it safe for Kevorkian or Adkins to assume she really did have Alzheimer's disease? Mendez recently published a study in which he examined the accuracy of diagnoses of Alzheimer's against autopsy findings in 846 cases. Depending on how generously the clinical definition of Alzheimer's is drawn, from 25 percent to 40 percent of those diagnosed as having Alzheimer's did not. Some of the conditions which can mimic the symptoms of Alzheimer's —brain tumors, fluid on the brain, metabolic diseases, stroke and depression — can be treated.

Did Adkins know that even if she did have Alzheimer's, the course of the disease varies greatly from person to person? Did she realize that she might have had many years of productive and dignified life ahead of her before the devastating effects of the disease set in? Did Kevorkian talk about any of this with her and her family?

PROSECUTION, NOT PRAISE

Kevorkian is being hailed as the man who at least had the guts to bring the topic of assisted euthanasia into the open. He should not be hailed, he should be indicted. He helped someone die under circumstances that would be comic if they were not so tragic. This death is an excellent starting point for an examination of why we are so blinded by our fears of disability, dying and death. Why can't we see that what Kevorkian did with Janet Adkins merits not praise but prosecution?

6 DR. KEVORKIAN AND ASSISTED SUICIDE

A MINISTER OF SELF-DELIVERANCE

Camille Kudzia

Camille Kudzia is the Vice President of the Hemlock Society of the upper Midwest. The Hemlock Society favors the legalization of physician-assisted suicide and active voluntary euthanasia.

Points to Consider:

1. How does Jack Kevorkian eliminate fear of a "botched suicide" by a debilitated person?

2. How is the feminist cause embraced by the Hemlock Society?

3. Explore the fact that those who have chosen Kevorkian's suicide methods have been mainly women.

4. What legislation is advocated by the Hemlock Society?

Camille Kudzia, "Users of Kevorkian Machine Saw It as Self-Deliverance," **Star Tribune**, July 4, 1992. Reprinted with permission from **Star Tribune**, Minneapolis.

For many people contemplating suicide, their greatest fear is a botched attempt.

"Why did she have to hang herself? Couldn't she have taken sleeping pills or poison?"

Such questions were posed over and over about my friend, a nurse who had taken care of many cancer patients and had attended her father, mother and sister as each died an agonizing death from the dread disease. A year before her death she, too, had been diagnosed with cancer.

She first may have tried suicide with sleeping pills. It was said she accidentally took an overdose a week before her death. Accident or botched suicide? What could be more devastating than to try to end one's life, and awake to find one had failed?

CONTEMPLATING SUICIDE

My friend was driven to desperate means because there was no legal way for her to do it otherwise. Her death occurred in the days before there were societies openly discussing this issue.

The Hemlock Society of the Upper Midwest often gets calls from people contemplating suicide. Their greatest fear is a botched attempt. They endure a bleak loneliness in reaching their decision. Generally all they want is someone to talk to — someone with an open mind.

Recently a 90-year-old woman called. A year ago she could walk three-quarters of a mile every day. When she was no longer able because of a sudden, weakened condition, she learned that she had cancer. She assessed her past existence, calculated that her long years had been well spent, and thus decided to quit life. She failed in her attempt because she did not take a strong enough draft of poison, was discovered, and revived. Now she says the beautiful independence she had enjoyed during her long life has disappeared. Her family watches over her constantly. Her impending death is doomed to a painful end.

In managing our own lives, we strive for the right of independence and the right of control. Ellen Goodman's May 26, 1992, column in the *Star Tribune* raises questions about these rights. "Janet, Sherry, Marjorie and Susan" may have been asserting their independence and control over their lives just as the 90-year-old woman was, and just as my friend who hanged herself may have been.

KEVORKIAN

Goodman's abhorrence of Jack Kevorkian is shared by many. He appears to have rubbed most people the wrong way, including the medical community and some members of the Hemlock Society. But the right of choice of "Janet, Sherry, Marjorie and Susan" should be carefully weighed. Before pontificating, one should consider the chances for a botched suicide in their debilitating state of health. Undoubtedly they wanted a method that was sure and fast. Kevorkian afforded this. If it is his means to death which repels some people, then it might be wise for them to work for a more cosmetically acceptable way.

It is implied that "Janet, Sherry, Marjorie and Susan" would still be here if there hadn't been a Jack Kevorkian and his death machine. Yes, Janet Adkins would be here degrading into an ever deeper presenile dementia. Sherry Miller and Susan Williams would be here with their distorted bodies degenerating into complete dependency. Marjorie Wanz would be here tormented by ever-present pain. Would Goodman wish such a horrible fate on any of these women?

FEMINISTS

Goodman has done a great deal for the feminist cause, but she is not the only feminist. In the Hemlock Society there are many women who are civil libertarians and who carry on the struggle for women's rights. They have been in the forefront in the battle for a woman's right to control her body. The struggle has been extended to the hopelessly ill to safeguard their right to remain in control of their bodies and to affirm their right, if they so wish, to quit life at a time of their own choosing.

Nor do our feminists agree with Goodman that "Janet, Sherry, Marjorie and Susan" were clinging vines easily persuaded by Kevorkian to use his machine. Rather they think of them as gutsy, determined women who did not want to risk a botched suicide and were not afraid to resort to the only sure method available to them.

"None of them were terminally ill," said the media accounts. True, but what chance would they have had to control their destiny if they had lingered? They preferred death to the existence

Life-support system

Cartoon by David Seavey. Copyright 1989, **USA Today**. Reprinted with permission.

awaiting them, and no one has the right to be judgmental about their decision.

Goodman is up in arms because most of those who have chosen death by Kevorkian's methods have been women. Hemlock regards this as a coincidence. If anything it could indicate that women are more courageous about facing the unknown than men. Moreover, far from being fickle about making this decision, the most important anyone can make, it might suggest that women are more resolute.

CONCLUSION

There is much to be done in the realm of civil liberties. When a method of self-deliverance is available to the hopelessly ill who wish it, when the method is guaranteed to be painless and sure, when one has the assurance that privacy will be strictly respected, and when one has been guaranteed that friends and family whose presence and help are desired will not be implicated as criminals, we will have gained a measure of independence and control over our lives. This the cause Hemlock espouses.

Since Kevorkian irritates Goodman, perhaps she could lend her pen to the above cause and support legislation that would make Kevorkian's machine obsolete.

7 DR. KEVORKIAN AND ASSISTED SUICIDE

A SERIAL KILLER ON THE LOOSE

Pat Buchanan

Patrick Buchanan is a nationally syndicated journalist. The follow-
ing article appeared in The Conservative Chronicle, *a weekly pub-*
lication based in Des Moines, Iowa.

Points to Consider:

1. Summarize Buchanan's opinion of Dr. Kevorkian.

2. What is Holland's policy on euthanasia?

3. Contrast: "sanctity of life" vs "quality of life".

4. How do New Age beliefs influence the assisted suicide decision?

Pat Buchanan, "Smiling Jack Kevorkian: Face of the Future," **The Conservative
Chronicle**, 1993. Reprinted with permission: Tribune Media Services.

Smiling Jack is a terminator, a serial mercy killer of the suicidally depressed.

Jack Kevorkian, the pathologist who made himself famous for assisting in 15 suicides, mostly of depressed women, may have gotten carried away with enthusiasm for his work.

A right-to-life activist discovered in a garbage bag outside the scene of several of Dr. K's suicides, his signed "Final Action" report on the death of No. 13, Hugh Gale.

Seventy-year-old Gale, suffering from emphysema and heart disease, volunteered to be gassed on February 15. According to the "Final Action", however, 45 seconds after Gale pulled the death mask over his face and started the flow of lethal carbon monoxide, he "became flushed, agitated, breathing deeply saying, 'Take it off.'"

Kevorkian complied. Twenty minutes later, Gale asked that the mask be put back on. "(He) again flushed, became agitated . . . and said, 'Take it off,' once again." This time, the mask was left on.

A police raid on Kevorkian's apartment found an updated "Final Action" with Gale's second "Take it off" whited out. With a county prosecutor mulling charges, and Michigan enacting a law making it a felony to assist suicide, Dr. Death's run may be over.

A "NUT CASE"

Kevorkian himself appears more than a bit of a nut case. As far back as the 1950s, writes Rita Marker of the International Anti-Euthanasia Task Force, Kevorkian had a grand plan to anesthetize death row inmates, to harvest their body parts while they were still alive.

His life has been spent around corpses. For two decades, he traveled California, living out of the same Volkswagen van where his first "patient" would kill herself. "During a stint at Beverly Hills Medical Center," writes an *L.A. Times* reporter, he was known for his "death rounds . . . He would rush to the bedsides of dying patients throughout the hospital to photograph their eyes to pinpoint the exact moment of death." Returning to Michigan, he advertised as a "Doctor-Consultant — for the terminally ill who wish to die."

Cartoon by Gary Markstein. Reprinted with permission of **The Milwaukee Journal**.

While Kevorkian's first victim was a woman in the early stages of Alzheimer's, another was a mental patient who complained of horrible pelvic pains, though an autopsy showed no sign of active disease.

"Now, the stage is set for fun!" Kevorkian whooped, on hearing Michigan had passed a law outlawing assisted suicide. In a taped discussion of one double suicide, Kevorkian is heard reassuring the grieving families, "They'll make the five o'clock news."

Kevorkian is not a doctor; he is not a friend, counselor, or healer of the sick. He has no expertise in treating cancer, heart disease, emphysema, Alzheimer's or multiple sclerosis, the real maladies of his "patients". Smiling Jack is a terminator, a serial mercy killer of the suicidally depressed, a disgrace to medicine who belongs in a padded cell or a prison dorm with the convicted killers whose vital organs this defrocked quack was once so anxious to collect.

"You pass any law against euthanasia or assisted suicide, and I will disobey it," says Dr. Death.

THE LAW

Appalled at his scoff-law attitude and tinker-toy death engines, Michigan recoiled. But Dr. K has put issues on the table that are not going away. "You have brought to the world's attention the need to give this topic paramount concern," said a judge in his first trial.

Holland agrees. Doctors who follow set procedure to assist the terminally ill to end their lives will no longer be prosecuted. One in every 50 deaths in Holland is a mercy killing. Reportedly, doctors are now taking it upon themselves to accelerate the departure of the terminally ill and elderly who are unwilling to go.

Outside Kevorkian's apartment this weekend, demonstrators carried signs saying, "Hit the Road, Jack" and "Send Jack to Jail." Others held signs reading, "Dr. K is OK," "Death with Dignity" and "Gas Engler" — John Engler, the Republican governor who signed the Michigan law outlawing assisted suicide.

The sign-carriers represent two sides of this ongoing debate in the West: The Sanctity of Life vs The Quality of Life.

Kevorkian and his Dutch allies have entered a post-Christian era that resembles the pre-Christian pagan era, when not all life was worth living, and suicide was an honorable way out. Their logic is inherent in Roe vs Wade: If a woman and her doctor can end the life of an unborn child, who are these "religious fanatics" to tell her she cannot end a life too painful to live? Whose life is it anyway?

THE NEW AGE

In the Old and New Testament, Augustine and Aquinas, natural law and Judeo-Christian tradition, God is the author of life; He has written the rules of human conduct in His words, His Books, and on the human heart; no man is permitted to play God, and take innocent life.

But, in the New Age, that is the old dogma of a dead creed. God does not exist. If He does, He is not party to the debate. Each of us, individually, determines his own moral code; and we will decide, democratically, of course, when life begins, and when it should end.

Because these conflicting beliefs are deeply held, compromise

DOCTOR DEATH

Janet, Sherry, Marjorie and Susan were not terminal by accepted medical definitions. Janet, Sherry, Marjorie and Susan — is it a coincidence that they are all women? — were not Kevorkian's patients in any traditional sense. He has no more right to wander around Michigan offering death to ill women than he has to put loaded guns in the hands of depressed teenagers.

As ethicist George Annas of Boston University says sharply, "He doesn't have a doctor-patient relationship with these people. He's not there for treatment or diagnosis. He doesn't give them alternatives or reasons to live. He's there to help you die." The only question now, says Annas, is "whether he should be in a mental institution or a prison."

Ellen Goodman, "Stop Dr. Death," **Boston Globe**, May, 1992

is impossible; one or the other will prevail in law, and determine the character of the people and nation we shall become.

Any man or woman who has chosen Jack Kevorkian as a death-bed doctor is suffering in soul as well as body, not only from disease but from despair. But despair is curable, and hope is the antidote, available at no cost. We need not only lock up Jack, but rescue his "patients", and tell them there is a better way out, more worthy of the children of a loving God, and a better world, on the other side.

8 DR. KEVORKIAN AND ASSISTED SUICIDE

ARE LAWS AGAINST ASSISTED SUICIDE UNCONSTITUTIONAL?

The ACLU vs The State of Michigan

The American Civil Liberties Union (ACLU) is a non-partisan organization with more than 275,000 members devoted to protecting the Bill of Rights.

Points to Consider:

1. According to the State of Michigan, what is the basic purpose for which governments are formed?

2. Comment: "It is the interest of the State...to protect the lives of those who wish to live no matter what their circumstances."

3. According to the ACLU, what do the due process clause and right of privacy guarantee offer the terminally ill?

4. Comment: "an absolute prohibition on a competent terminally ill person's choice...is the most extreme undue burden..."

Excerpted from legal arguments by the Michigan ACLU and the State of Michigan before the Michigan Court of Appeals, June 2, 1993. In this case, Dr. Jack Kevorkian was being accused of murder by the State of Michigan.

The Point

This statute addresses the topic of assisted suicide. The clear objective is to regulate this area in order to protect the legitimate interest of society.

NANCY CRUZAN

In Cruzan vs Director, the United States Supreme Court found that a person has a constitutionally protected interest in refusing unwanted medical treatment or procedures. The court also affirmed the state's power to keep an incompetent, vegetative patient alive where that person had not left clear instructions for ending life-sustaining treatment.

Cruzan does not support a conclusion that there is a constitutionally-protected "right to die". Neither the opinion of the Court, written by Chief Justice Rehnquist, nor the dissent implied that any recognition of a right to refuse unwanted medical procedures was tantamount to a right to commit suicide. The Opinion of the Court further cites the fact that a majority of the states have criminally prohibited assisted suicide with no suggestion that such laws are constitutionally suspect.

Refusal of life-sustaining medical treatment is fundamentally different from a suicide. Suicide is defined as: "the act or an instance of taking one's own life voluntarily and intentionally; the deliberate and intentional destruction of his own life by a person of years of discretion and of sound mind; one that commits or attempts self-murder."

SUICIDE

Even assuming that due process liberty extends to an individual's decision to commit suicide, it certainly does not follow that someone who aids or assists the implementation of this decision cannot be held criminally responsible. Though no state has made suicide or attempted suicide a crime by enactment of statute, the majority of states in this country have laws imposing criminal penalties on one who assists another to commit suicide.

In People vs Roberts, 211 Mich 187; 178 NW 690 (1920), the Court affirmed the first degree murder conviction of a husband who assisted his wife's suicide by making a cup of deadly poison available to her. The Court rejected the husband's argument that, since suicide itself was not a crime, his act of assistance to his wife was also not a crime. In this regard, the Court stated:

"Where one person advises, aids, or abets another to commit suicide, and the other by reason thereof kills himself, and the adviser is present when he does so, he is guilty of murder as a principal, or in some jurisdictions of manslaughter; or if two persons mutually agree to kill themselves together, and the means employed to produce death take effect upon one only, the survivor is guilty of murder of the one who dies. But if the one who encourages another to commit suicide is not present when the act is done, he is an accessory before the act and at common law escapes punishment. The abolition of the distinction between aiders and accessories in some jurisdictions, has, however, carried away this distinction, so that a person may now be convicted of murder for advising a suicide, whether absent or present at the time it is committed, provided the suicide is the result of his advice."

The Roberts Court also made it clear that the direction or desires of the decedent did not absolve the one providing assistance.

In a 1993 decision, the Michigan Court of Appeals concluded that Roberts did not represent the current law of Michigan. In People vs Campbell, the Court concluded that the defendant had not possessed a present intention to kill but merely provided a weapon to the decedent and departed with the hope that the latter would kill himself. The Court questioned whether an "incitement to suicide" was a crime under the common law. In this regard, the Court noted that "while we find the conduct of the defendant morally reprehensible, we do not find it to be criminal under the present state of the law." There is no suggestion in Campbell, however, that the legislature would lack power to make such morally reprehensible conduct subject to criminal sanction.

Over the years, the Legislature has considered various proposals to make assisted suicide a separate and distinct offense. Legislation has also been introduced to permit physicians to assist in suicides under certain carefully defined circumstances.

CONCLUSION

Nothing in this history suggests a societal recognition of a right to have assistance for one's own suicide. Regardless of the legality of such conduct prior to the enactment of the present prohibition, it is clear that such behavior has long been considered morally reprehensible or at least undesirable. There is no fundamental right entitled to constitutional protection in these circumstances.

It is undisputable that the prohibition of assistance to a suicide is rationally related to a legitimate state interest. The state's interest in preserving life is both fundamental and compelling. It constitutes the basic purpose for which governments are formed. Specifically, the state has a legitimate interest in preventing suicides.

This interest is more significant than merely the abstract interest in preserving life no matter what the quality of that life is. Instead, it is the interest of the state to maintain social order through enforcement of the criminal law and to protect the lives of those who wish to live no matter what their circumstances.

Given the potential for abuse that can exist in an assisted suicide situation, a legislative decision to prohibit such activity cannot be deemed irrational.

The Counterpoint

ACLU

The sweeping prohibitions against "assisted suicide" contained in the statute impose an "undue burden" on the terminally ill person's fundamental right of personal autonomy by prohibiting physicians from prescribing medications which a terminally ill person may use to hasten inevitable death, and by prohibiting any other person from providing assistance to the terminally ill person in administering and ingesting those medications.

PAIN AND SUFFERING

In denying that the interests of a terminally ill person in hastening his or her inevitable death in order to end continuing and unbearable pain and suffering are constitutionally protected, the State of Michigan insists that such action amounts to a "suicide", and so is "fundamentally different from refusal of life-sustaining medical treatment." This attempt to put the pejorative label "suicide" on a terminally ill person's choice to hasten his or her inevitable death by ingesting physician-prescribed medications simply begs the question and cannot constitute a constitutionally valid justification for the statute's drastic interference with the terminally ill person's fundamental right of personal autonomy. In no meaningful sense can a terminally ill person's choice to hasten his or her inevitable death by the use of physician-prescribed medications be labeled a "suicide". The term "suicide" conjures up the image of a person jumping off a bridge or "blowing his brains out." The terminally ill person who is facing death, and who seeks to have the choice to hasten inevitable death by the use of physician-prescribed medications, is not "committing suicide" by ending a life that otherwise is of indefinite duration. Quite to the contrary, the "life" of the terminally ill person is coming to an end, and the only question is whether the terminally ill person must undergo unbearable pain and suffering until death comes "naturally", or whether that person can make the choice to end the unbearable pain and suffering by the use of physician-prescribed medications. The question of whether the Michigan and United States Constitutions protect the right of the terminally ill person to have this choice cannot be "preempted" or circumvented by saying that the person is "committing suicide" and so cannot claim constitutional protection for this right.

PERSONAL AUTONOMY

Rather the question of whether the Michigan and United States Constitutions protect the right of the competent terminally ill person to have this choice must be answered with reference to the constitutional doctrine relating to the right of personal autonomy that has been promulgated by the United States and Michigan Supreme Courts. Quite astonishingly, the State never discusses this constitutional doctrine. It never mentions the United States Supreme Court's recent Casey decision or the long line of Michigan Supreme Court decisions holding that an essential component of the generic right to privacy derived from the Michigan Constitution is a person's ability to control his or her own body. Nor does the State ever explain any principled difference between the right of a competent terminally ill person to hasten inevitable death by refusing to continue life-sustaining medical treatment, and the right of the same competent terminally ill person to hasten inevitable death by the use of physician-prescribed medications, and there is none.

It is perhaps well to recall at this juncture the United States Supreme Court's ringing affirmation of the right of personal autonomy in Casey: "It is a promise of the Constitution that there is a realm of person liberty which the government may not enter...It is settled now...that the Constitution places limits on a State's right to interfere with a person's most basic decisions about family and parenthood, as well as bodily integrity... At the heart of liberty is the right to define one's own concept of existence, of the meaning of the universe, and of the mystery of human life.

Competent terminally ill persons have the right to make the "most basic decisions about bodily integrity." They have the right to "define [their] own concept of existence" and "the attributes of [their] personhood," without the "compulsion of the State." They have the right to make the choice whether to continue to undergo unbearable pain and suffering until death comes "naturally", or to hasten inevitable death by the use of physician-prescribed medications. The right to make this choice is surely a fundamental right, protected by the due process clauses of the United States and Michigan Constitutions and by the right of privacy guarantee derived from the Michigan Constitution.

Casey also holds that the government may not impose an undue burden on the exercise of a person's fundamental right to bodily integrity and control of one's own body. An absolute prohibition on a competent terminally ill person's choice to use physician-prescribed medications to hasten inevitable death is the most extreme undue burden on the exercise of a fundamental right that is possible to imagine, and under Casey is clearly unconstitutional.

CONCLUSION

The ban on the use of physician-prescribed medications by a competent terminally ill person to hasten inevitable death does not advance any interest in "preserving life". Quite to the contrary, it does nothing more than force the terminally ill person to undergo continued unbearable pain and suffering, and the State can have no conceivably valid interest in preventing competent terminally ill persons from ending their misery by using physician-prescribed medications to hasten their inevitable death.

The statute's absolute prohibition on the choice of competent terminally ill persons to hasten their inevitable death by the use of physician-prescribed medications imposes an undue burden on the exercise of the fundamental right of personal autonomy, and so is patently unconstitutional.

EXAMINING COUNTERPOINTS

This activity may be used as an individualized study guide for students in libraries and resource centers or as a discussion catalyst in small group and classroom discussions.

The Point

Physician-assisted suicide should be permitted under a humane and dignified death act where the patient has signed a request wishing to die. A second medical opinion would be mandatory and the family would have to be informed. Doctors who disagree with a patient's request would not be obliged to help but must free the person to seek a more sympathetic doctor.

The Counterpoint

Bringing on death can never be right. Physician-assisted suicide "is putting to death" with the doctor as executioner. Euthanasia is capital punishment for the crime of being elderly, disabled or ill. And it is wrong whatever the circumstances. Euthanasia is a deadly game that could lead to the excesses Germany experienced under Hitler.

• • • •

The Point

Doctors should be permitted to assist in terminating a patient's life but should never be allowed to directly take action that would end a life.

The Counterpoint

It should be legal for doctors to take direct action to end a patient's life when there is no hope for a cure and the patient requests a merciful end to needless suffering.

Guidelines

Part A

Examine the counterpoints above and then consider the following questions.

1. Do you agree more with the point or counterpoint in each case? Why?

2. Which reading in Chapter Two best illustrates the point in each case?

3. Which reading best illustrates each counterpoint?

4. Do any cartoons in this publication illustrate the meaning of the point or counterpoint arguments? Which ones and why?

Part B

Social issues are usually complex, but often problems become oversimplified in political debates and discussions. Usually a polarized version of social conflict does not adequately represent the diversity of views that surround social conflict. Examine the counterpoints above. Then write down other possible interpretations.

CHAPTER 3

EUTHANASIA IN THE NETHERLANDS

9   EUTHANASIA IN THE NETHERLANDS

ASSISTED SUICIDE AND EUTHANASIA IN THE NETHERLANDS:
An Overview

Dick Polman

Dick Polman is a staff writer for The Philadelphia Inquirer.

Points to Consider:

1. Summarize the 28 official guidelines that Netherlands doctors must follow in performing euthanasia.

2. How strongly do Dutch citizens favor permitting euthanasia?

3. How might the practice of euthanasia lead to a "slippery slope", making it easier for doctors to kill without consent?

4. Why are the Dutch guidelines requiring "unbearable suffering" which might be physical or mental, such a dilemma for doctors?

Dick Polman, "For the Dutch, Life's End Can Be a Matter of Choice," reprinted with permission of **The Philadelphia Inquirer**, April 4, 1993.

"This is a very significant step," said J.K.M. Gevers, a health law professor at the Amsterdam Medical Center, **"because the government has now officially committed itself to the practice of euthanasia."**

Utrecht, Netherlands — With each passing sunset, he lost his grip on the small pleasures of life. His taste buds went. Then, his stamina. Then, his ability to swallow. Then, his love of reading. Then, his mental acuity.

One year after Anton van't Hoenderdaal was told of his incurable cancer, he had only two things left: his ability to vomit, and his sense of dignity. He didn't care about the first, but he did want to preserve the second. So one afternoon in October, he called his son Bert to his bedroom, and said, "I don't want to go on like this anymore."

Bert knew what that meant. Anton had always been the boss of the family, an autocrat of willful pride, and it was clear that he didn't want to die like a dog. He had seen it happen too many times, back in the war, as a prisoner of the Nazis.

So Bert did what the Dutch often do in such circumstances. He told the family doctor that his father wished to be put to sleep, forever. The medical term is euthanasia, which is administered here roughly 3,000 times a year, in three percent of all deaths. But Bert calls it common sense — as does the Dutch government, which recently enacted the most liberal euthanasia law in the world.

"I was very happy that he could decide when to die," said Bert, a psychotherapist, "instead of him slowly going into a coma and us not knowing how long it would take. He always wanted to control his life. The idea of helplessness was unbearable for him. So the way he was able to leave, it suited his character."

What Anton requested, and what his doctor soon performed, was a criminal act. Even today, what the Ministry of Justice defines as "active medical intervention to cut short life, at the express request of the patient," remains a crime.

NEW LAW

But under the law enacted in February, doctors who commit that crime are guaranteed immunity — as long as they follow cer-

61

tain rules.

"This is a very significant step," said J.K.M. Gevers, a health law professor at the Amsterdam Medical Center, "because the government has now officially committed itself to the practice of euthanasia."

Under the new law, doctors who perform euthanasia are supposed to report their cases to the government. Then they must show that they have followed 28 official guidelines: in essence, that the patient asked for death without any prompting, that the patient was suffering unbearably with no hope for reprieve, and that the doctor had sought a second opinion from a colleague.

Actually, this has been the practice in the Netherlands for years, but without the government's blessing. Gevers pointed out the new paradox: "On one hand, euthanasia will remain a crime," punishable by 12 years in prison. "On the other hand, the same doctor will not be prosecuted if he carefully commits that crime."

Many doctors still resent the implication that they are presumed guilty until they can prove their innocence. They are also anxious to dispel fears that the Dutch are eager to snuff out the lives of handicapped babies, coma patients and cranky seniors.

"Helping a patient die is never good medical practice. It's only the best of two bad possibilities," said Herbert Cohen, a balding and bearded doctor who practices — and has performed euthanasia — near Rotterdam. "Good medical practice is to cure someone so they can go skiing. People who oppose euthanasia assume the choice is always between dying and living happily ever after. But sometimes, it's just a choice between two ways of dying."

"I do it once every couple of years. It gives me many sleepless nights whenever I do it...That's the way it should be. If euthanasia ever becomes easy, that's when you should be checked out by somebody."

The Dutch favor permitting euthanasia — 78 percent in a recent poll — but the practice attracts vociferous critics at home and abroad. A few weeks ago, Henk Ten Have, a medical ethics professor at Nymejen University, warned of a "slippery slope" that will make it easier for doctors to kill without consent. Walter Reich, a health policy scholar in Washington, said the new Dutch law "will have a corrupting effect on the value of life."

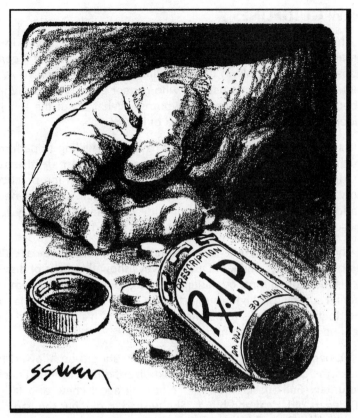

Cartoon by David Seavey. Copyright 1991, **USA Today**. Reprinted with permission.

"No, no, no," countered Pieter Admiraal, an anesthesiologist at Delft General Hospital. "It is an emotional thing to do euthanasia, very emotional. Every time, I lose a friend. I'm not just a doctor, I'm a humanistic human. Euthanasia brings you closer to the patient. It is not some crazy experiment, it is the most close relationship there ever is."

"Doctors only report the clear-cut cases," Cohen said. "If they're uncertain, they won't report it. They just tell the coroner, 'natural causes'. It's tricky, because the government wants to check on the practice. But with punishment still on the books, half the doctors don't report. And if they don't report, there's nothing for the government to check."

NEW GUIDELINES

The new law also has failed to satisfy those who believe in a broader definition of the right to die. While the government condones euthanasia only in cases of willful consent, others are asking: What about coma patients who cannot give consent? What about severely handicapped newborns? What about the lonely elderly citizens who are simply sick of living?

As a general rule, Dutch doctors have been willing to perform euthanasia only in cases of desperate physical illness. Traditionally, Dutch medical leaders have tolerated the practice only when the dying process has actually begun. But the new national guidelines appear to provide considerable leeway for those ostensibly healthy seniors who wish to end their lives.

The guidelines require "unbearable suffering", but physical pain is not mandatory. Indeed, Dutch surveys show that "loss of dignity" is mentioned most by patients seeking to die. The problem is, mental suffering is highly subjective — and a terrible dilemma for the doctor who wants to balance the wishes of his patient and the healing requirements of his profession.

"A person who is suffering emotionally should be allowed to make the choice," said Marion Rookhuizen, director of the Dutch Voluntary Euthanasia Society. "Not long ago I knew of a lady, 103 years old, deaf and blind. She wished to die, but she had no real illness. She said she couldn't go on.

For months, there were five different meetings, with doctors and psychiatrists, before it was agreed that she could get her wish."

As for coma patients, even allies differ on what to do. Herbert Cohen, the doctor, said flatly, "I won't help a relative who says, 'Put my sister out of her misery.' Well, is it misery for the patient? I don't know, and she can't tell me." But Marion Ebbinge, who helps euthanasia patients in Amsterdam, insisted, "After 28 days in a coma, a person will never be the same. If a relative thinks that person should die, she should die."

Meanwhile, roughly 10 times a year in the Netherlands, babies born with severe disabilities are allowed to die. In these cases of "newborn euthanasia", parents and doctors make the call. Gray areas abound. In one recent case, a newborn with Down's syndrome was denied treatment, because her parents wanted her to die. The attending doctor was investigated, but never prosecuted.

"I'm not sure I would have agreed with that absence of treatment," said Admiraal, the anesthesiologist, choosing his words carefully. "It was up to the parents." Indeed, the Dutch Pediatric Association, in an effort to protect its doctors from prosecution, is lobbying for separate guidelines on newborns.

FUNDAMENTAL QUESTIONS

All told, "euthanasia is still very difficult for us," said Gevers, the health law professor. "The fundamental question is simple. To what extent does society assert itself for the preservation of life? Or should you give way — very understandably, from a subjective view — to the individual preferences of people?"

But for Bert van't Hoenderdaal, it was all very pure. In his apartment the other day, he reminisced. The windowpanes were streaked with rain. Down the block, bells chimed in a 12th-century church tower.

"After my father told me he didn't want to live anymore, we had about five days until the doctor could come to the house," he said. "His decision made us more open, to talk about things you're not always open about. We focused on the time he chose to have left. The whole family was able to come and say goodbye."

Anton had been a social worker, the guy that straightened out everyone's problems. Now he sought to solve his own. In the last minute of life, Bert held his hand. The family doctor injected him with a heavy sedative; then, 10 seconds later, a lethal injection.

"It all went away, from one moment to the next," said Bert, still in awe. "His whole life, all the experiences he had, all the passions, all the purpose — to see 72 years disappear like that . . . What mattered was, he did it on his own terms, without being hooked to a machine."

He was left with an image of Anton as a war prisoner, forced by the Nazis to stand outside for hours on a winter's night, clad only in a linen shirt. His father, he decided, had survived indignity before.

And now he had done it again.

10   EUTHANASIA IN THE NETHERLANDS

CORRUPTING THE VALUE OF LIFE

Walter Reich

Walter Reich, a psychiatrist, is senior scholar and director of the Project on Health, Science and Public Policy at the Woodrow Wilson International Center for scholars. He wrote the following article for The New York Times.

Points to Consider:

1. What is the Hippocratic Oath and when and why was it written?

2. What might the impact of the Dutch euthanasia model be in undemocratic countries?

3. How does the author view preserving life artificially?

4. How might the practice of euthanasia change the identity of the physician?

Once doctors trained to preserve life are no longer afraid of initiating death — then the very nature of the medical enterprise, and the very identity of the physician, is changed.

The Parliament of the Netherlands, one of the most humane nations on earth, has given Dutch physicians, members of one of the most humane professions on earth, permission to kill their patients.

Physicians still have to follow rules. The patient must ask for death, must not be depressed when asking for it, must be well informed about his illness and options and must feel his suffering is unacceptable.

The physician must consult a colleague before doing the deed and, having done it, must inform the authorities why he was justified in doing it.

MERCY KILLINGS

In 1990, one out of 50 deaths in the Netherlands was the result of mercy killings carried out in a country in which ever more physicians were prepared to perform euthanasia and in which the authorities did not enforce existing laws against it.

Last year, the number of such killings rose markedly; now it may skyrocket. You don't have to be religious to mourn the new law. All you have to be is human and alive. All you have to understand is that a patient, no matter how ill or despondent, is still human and still alive, and that killing that patient,no matter what the law says or what the circumstances are, is still killing.

People kill without benefit of the law every day. Soldiers kill other soldiers legally. But societies can experience such killings and remain essentially decent. It's when they legalize the killings of their own innocent members that they remove an obstacle that blocks the all-too-easy slide of civilization into moral chaos. When they permit killing by medical means, they eviscerate the human essence of the medical enterprise.

DEMOCRACY

Is the Netherlands about to join Nazi Germany by sliding into the hell of Auschwitz? Hardly. Members of the Parliament who

Cartoon by Steve Bensen. Reprinted with permission: Tribune Media Services.

voted for the mercy killing bill did so out of powerful feelings of compassion for patients.

It's precisely because the Dutch have so exemplary a history of decency, and their parliamentarians so thorough a commitment to democracy, that the act is so troubling.

It provides a model for the easing by a democratic nation of the taboo against the legalized killing of innocent people — an easing girded by rules that seem tight now but that will be loosened, inevitably, in practice.

The spectacle of the formalized and regular killing of such patients — resulting not in one Dutch death out of 50 but in five deaths out of 50, or 10, or 20, or even more — will have a corrupting effect, not only on the value of life in the Netherlands but also in every other democratic country.

But the greatest impact of this spectacle may be in undemocratic countries, where authorities less humane than Dutch legislators may seize upon the Dutch example as a useful model without bothering to set up rules to guide physicians in their killing work.

They may even provide rules that permit, encourage or even demand all kinds of killing, beginning with the killing of people

LICENSE TO KILL

The Hippocratic Oath, written more than 2,000 years ago in response to a revulsion against the utilitarian motives behind abortion, infanticide and euthanasia in ancient Greece, established for the first time "a complete separation between killing and curing," in the words of the late anthropologist Margaret Mead. The oath, which was pagan in origin, would later be infused with ethical and moral principles contained in the Old and New Testaments.

Now that those principles are no longer regarded by many people as relevant for a modern age, we are regressing to that pre-Hippocrates time in which technique, skill and outcome, rather than intrinsic value, are to guide physicians as they determine who should live and who should die.

Cal Thomas, "Dutch Parliament Gives Doctors a License to Kill," **Los Angeles Times Syndicate**, February 14, 1993

who ask for it and progressing to the killing of people who are said to deserve it.

Doctors in the Netherlands, like doctors everywhere, are bound by millennia of solemn oath to preserve life. Their patients expect that commitment from them and the physicians expect it from themselves.

To be sure, it's a commitment that can get out of hand: Sometimes physicians preserve life artificially and mindlessly in a manner that, solely because of the work of machines, keeps the heart beating long after the brain has died.

But going overboard, when it's done out of a genuine desire to preserve life if even the smallest chance of recovery is possible, is an essentially noble act that, even if it is excessive, at least guards the central and classical values of medicine.

LIFE'S MISSION

However, once the medical commitment to life is undermined by legal sanction — once doctors trained to preserve life are no longer afraid of initiating death — then the very nature of the medical enterprise, and the very identity of the physician, is changed.

The doctor loses the mission of caring for life and takes on the role of an amoral medical technician, one whose duty could just as well be to end life as to preserve it. That's a profession that I want no part of. Society deserves better. And, most important of all, patients deserve better.

11 EUTHANASIA IN THE NETHERLANDS

PROTECTING THE VALUE OF LIFE

Hemlock Quarterly

The following article was excerpted from The Hemlock Quarterly, *a publication of the Hemlock Society, which promotes legalizing physician-assisted suicide and active voluntary euthanasia.*

Points to Consider:

1. How has the doctor / patient relationship changed in the last few decades?

2. What are the two main reasons patients request euthanasia?

3. Why, in Dr. Admiraal's hospital, is the family not involved in the euthanasia decision?

4. Who in the Netherlands must accept ultimate responsibility for euthanasia, and how is prosecution avoided?

Kristin Larson, "Euthanasia in a Dutch Hospital," **The Hemlock Quarterly**, October 1990. Reprinted with permission.

Only the patient can request euthanasia.

"Every patient has the right to judge his suffering as unbearable and the right to ask his doctor for euthanasia," said Dr. Pieter Admiraal at the 8th Biennial World Conference of Right to Die Societies held in Maastrict, the Netherlands.

Dr. Admiraal, an anesthesiologist, was the first physician in the Netherlands to speak openly about practicing euthanasia. In his speech he described the reasons he believes patients choose euthanasia and the procedure for carrying it out in the general hospital where he practices.

In his 40 year career, Admiraal has seen the doctor/patient relationship change. The patient no longer relinquishes all control to his doctor, but is involved in the decision making process until the end of life. This evolution has made self-determination an important factor in defining the course medical care takes in the Netherlands, and has led to the practice of active euthanasia for those who decide to end their lives in the face of a terminal illness.

THE CRITICS

Critics argue that pain is what drives people to choose euthanasia; Admiraal, however, said that pain is rarely a reason for euthanasia in his hospital. "The presumption that patients who are in agonizing pain ask for euthanasia as a last resort is correct, but the reverse assumption that with proper pain treatment a patient never will ask for euthanasia is incorrect. The main reasons patients request euthanasia, stated Admiraal, are the loss of dignity that may accompany the final stages of terminal illness and the acceptance that death is inevitable.

Admiraal believes the suffering of one human being cannot be judged by another — each patient reacts to an end of life situations differently, and all care for the dying patient is based on the patient's own view of death and dying. It is wrong to call one patient "heroic" who suffers through the last stages of terminal illness and then refer to another as "cowardly" because he or she chooses euthanasia.

PATIENT REQUEST

When a patient requests euthanasia, and about 10% of the terminal patients in Admiraal's hospital do, the first step is to

improve palliative care in hopes that euthanasia may be avoided. If this does not lessen the emotional or physical discomfort of the patient, doctors, nurses, and clergy discuss the euthanasia option, each having an equal say in the decision making process. Any member of the decision making "team" has the right to refuse cooperation in a case of euthanasia, but this refusal cannot stop euthanasia from taking place.

The family may offer spiritual input, but is not involved in the final decision. Nor can a family request euthanasia for a family member — only the patient can request euthanasia. (Also, in a written request, a patient may ask that his/her family never be told about the euthanasia.) This protects the patient in two ways; the family cannot force euthanasia upon the patient and the family cannot prevent euthanasia if the patient insists on it.

THE LAW

Euthanasia is illegal in the Netherlands, but if doctors follow a strict set of legal requirements the chances of prosecution are

AN ETHICAL VIEW

Even if we doubt the point of continuing treatment in cases where the patient wants no more, and where it seems best to let in death it is quite a different matter to cross the line and to actively bring about death. Many feel that man should not cross this line. Others feel that euthanasia —administered under strict conditions — is an act of ultimate compassion that fits very well in the doctor's duty to stand by his patient in his most difficult hour. It is not a matter doctors think lightly about, for the act is irreversible and by its very nature completely different from any other medical act.

A leading Dutch ethicist, Dr. H. Kuitert, expresses it this way: if suffering has become so terrible and so unbearable that human life as it were sinks through the bottom of a minimum of human dignity, the patient involved has a definite case to ask for euthanasia. This ultimate deed of his doctor, if granted, does not cause harm to him but is beneficial in the full sense of the word.

J. Kits Nienwenkamp, a Position Paper from The Dutch Ministry of Information, 1992

small. These requirements are: 1) The patient has been fully informed of his/her condition and chances for recovery. 2) The doctor must be convinced that the patient freely requests euthanasia and has carefully considered this option. 3) The doctor, after thorough investigation, believes that euthanasia is justified. 4) Another doctor has been consulted. 5) The doctor keeps the medical record for five years. 6) The guardians of patients under 16 years of age have been consulted unless there is sufficient good reason not to.

In addition to these legal requirements, Dr. Admiraal's hospital has further criteria for euthanasia. First, a patient must sign a declaration requesting euthanasia. A written report which includes all relevant information regarding the request for euthanasia is made. And finally a "checklist" which outlines the process leading to the decision to perform euthanasia must be signed by two doctors.

The doctor must accept ultimate responsibility for the euthanasia and if a doctor decides to perform euthanasia, the medical director of the hospital is informed anonymously. The coroner is then notified that an unnatural death has occurred and an autopsy is performed. The checklist and the patient's proclamation are sent to the prosecutor.

Admiraal believes that euthanasia is the ultimate act of terminal care. "Without terminal care," he said, "there is no euthanasia and there is no terminal care without the possibility of euthanasia." In his hospital respect for self-determination, respect for the caregiver, and respect for the law are primary.

12   EUTHANASIA IN THE NETHERLANDS

EUTHANASIA:
The Medicine of Death and Fear

Richard Fenigsen

.

Richard Fenigsen, M.D., Ph.D., a Dutch citizen, is a retired cardiologist who has lectured and published widely.

Points to Consider:

1. According to the 1990 Dutch Committee, what percent of deaths are by euthanasia?

2. Summarize Dutch data regarding involuntary euthanasia.

3. How well are the officially accepted guidelines for euthanasia being followed?

4. Comment: "Hippocratic medicine's truthful, modest attitude has become obsolete."

Richard Fenigsen, "A Gentle Man Speaks of Fear," **Living World**, 1992. Reprinted with permission of the author and **Living World** Magazine.

The report showed that the situation is worse than the opponents of euthanasia ever suspected.

The debate on the issue of euthanasia is now going on in many countries including the United States, but only in Holland is active euthanasia, injecting sick people with drugs that cause death, widely and openly practiced. What does it mean for the people involved, and for all people? Has the practice of euthanasia changed the medical profession and society?

EUTHANASIA IN HOLLAND

At present, Holland is the only place you can look for answers to these questions. But, the truth about Dutch euthanasia has long been the subject of controversy.

The defenders of euthanasia, in particular in the United States, say look, Holland is a democratic nation of decent, reasonable people. They have allowed active euthanasia and this has now been going on some twenty years with no bad consequences whatsoever. Euthanasia in Holland is not formally legalized, but the official guidelines strictly regulate the practice and provide good safeguards against abuse. The freedom and the rights of people have been expanded; they include now the choice of death, and dying patients who are in intractable pain can now be put out of their misery.

However, the critics of Dutch euthanasia always asserted that it is practiced on a very large scale, not only in terminal cases, but also on people with various chronic ailments, or with psychological disorders; that many doctors arbitrarily terminate patients' lives without the patients' request, consent, or knowledge; and that irregularities and misdemeanors are the rule rather than the exception. The critics have also alleged that euthanasia frightens whole groups of the population, and corrupts the legal system, family ties, and the whole fabric of society. Which picture is true?

GOVERNMENT COMMITTEE'S REPORT

The controversy around Dutch euthanasia is now resolved. In 1990, the Committee to Investigate the Medical Practice Concerning Euthanasia appointed by the Dutch government ordered a nationwide survey of the practice of euthanasia. Very reliable methods of study were adopted and the researchers working for the Committee have taken every effort to obtain full and truthful information.

When the Committee's report was released on Sept. 10, 1991, in two volumes, it immediately became clear that it contains the most valuable and extensive information on Dutch euthanasia. Now there is no more controversy about the facts.

And which side in the debate proved right? Has the report confirmed the allegations of the critics of euthanasia? Yes, indeed, and more than that. The report showed that the situation is worse than the opponents of euthanasia ever suspected. Here I want to pay tribute to the Dutch researchers. The people who did this study and members of the governmental committee support euthanasia. They have tried to reduce the impact of the report by including some reassuring comments and conclusions. But they showed honesty and courage by publishing all the findings however alarming they turned out to be.

How many people die by euthanasia in Holland every year? To calculate this from the report, we first have to agree on the definition of euthanasia. There are good grounds to adopt a descriptive definition which includes all essential forms of euthanasia. Professor Joseph Fletcher, now deceased, who was a prominent advocate of euthanasia, proposed such a definition that I present here in my own wording: Euthanasia means deliberately causing the death of a person either by action or by omission with or without the request of the person involved, and with the professed aim of sparing that person the suffering of illness or an imperfect life.

EVERY FIFTH PERSON DIES OF EUTHANASIA

When we apply Fletcher's definition to the data supplied in the Dutch report, we see that the number of people who die by euthanasia in the Netherlands is more than 25,000 a year. This is 19.4 percent of all deaths. In other words, every fifth death in the country is due to euthanasia. [The total figure of 25,000 cases must be supplemented by a presumably not very large number of handicapped newborn, sick children, psychiatric patients, and patients with AIDS, as, according to the report, termination of life is practiced in these cases as well, but no quantitative estimates have been obtained.]

In 13,000 cases, passive euthanasia has been performed, which means the death was caused by withholding or withdrawing life saving treatment. In 12,000 cases, active euthanasia was carried

Cartoon by David Seavey. Copyright 1985, **USA Today**. Reprinted with permission.

out; that means the patients were killed by administering drugs which caused cardiac-respiratory arrest. Twenty-five thousand cases of euthanasia a year is a huge number. Holland's population is now 15 million. If euthanasia occurred in America with the same frequency as in Holland, this would amount to 400,000 cases of euthanasia a year for the United States. If active euthanasia were practiced in America with the same frequency, it would amount to 190,000 cases a year for the United States.

The report contains many other very interesting data. In 1990, when the study was done, the Dutch doctors rejected 6,700 requests for euthanasia which indicates, in the Committee's opinion, that such requests are seriously considered and not too easily granted. However, according to a parallelly conducted study, when the request for euthanasia is granted, in 59% of the cases euthanasia is carried out on the day of the request. And in 11% of cases, *within one hour* of the request, which suggests not so much a dutiful consideration, but rather an unseemly haste.

Euthanasia is not limited to patients in terminal condition. According to the doctors' own assessments, in 21% of the cases euthanasia shortened the patients' lives by one to six months; in 8% of cases, by more than six months. Further, the handicapped newborn babies and the psychiatric patients are certainly not terminal, and yet, euthanasia is practiced in these cases.

EUTHANASIA WITHOUT CONSENT

The report of the governmental committee is the first official acknowledgement that involuntary euthanasia is practiced in Holland. According to the data published in the report, 14,691 people died in 1990 by involuntary euthanasia, which means that these lives were cut short by the doctors without the request, consent, or knowledge of the patients. When this occurs in the hospital, in 45% of the cases, euthanasia is carried out not only without the knowledge of the patients but also without the knowledge of the family.

The death of 8,750 persons was caused by withdrawing life-prolonging treatment without the patients' knowledge. And the lives of 5,941 persons were actively terminated without the involved persons' consent or knowledge by administering lethal injections. Fourteen hundred persons who underwent active, involuntary euthanasia were fully competent. In 8% of cases, the doctors proceeded to perform active involuntary euthanasia while they believed that other courses of action were still possible. "Low quality of life," "no prospect of improvement," and "the family could not take it any more" were among the most frequently cited reasons to terminate the patients' lives without their consent.

So it happens in Holland, that when a person is admitted to a hospital people are supposed to trust, a doctor will evaluate the quality of his life, will make up his mind, and without asking the patient whether he wishes this or not, will give him an injection which stops his breathing and heartbeat. One Dutchman out of 22 dies in this way.

Let's make it clear; some of the patients whose lives were cut short without their consent or knowledge, were incompetent, unconscious. Some of them were fully competent, not partially,

but fully competent patients who, according to the doctors themselves, could well evaluate their own situation and make decisions, and in spite of that, they were not asked about their own
wishes and their lives were terminated by doctors. According to
the report, 1,474 — fully competent — patients underwent involuntary euthanasia.

GUIDELINES WIDELY DISREGARDED

So the report of the governmental committee is the first official
acknowledgement that involuntary euthanasia is practiced in
Holland, not as some sporadic act committed by outcasts, but as
part of regular medical practice. The report also shows that the
rules of so-called careful conduct officially accepted as guidelines
for euthanasia are widely disregarded by the physicians.

In cases of voluntary euthanasia, 19% of the general practitioners disregard the rule to consult another physician. Sixty percent
of the general practitioners do not consult another physician
before carrying out involuntary active euthanasia. And 54% omit
to record the proceedings in writing, which is one of the rules. In
the death certificates, 72% of doctors conceal the fact that the
patient died by voluntary euthanasia. In cases of active involuntary euthanasia, the doctors, with a single exception, *never* stated
the truth on the death certificates.

The total number of cases in which the death is deliberately
hastened by action or omission, is perhaps the most striking finding published in the report. There were 130,000 deaths in
Holland in 1990. Of these, 43,000 people died suddenly due to
accidents or sudden cardiac death, and this precluded any medical decisions about the end of life in the wording of the report.
Of the remaining 86,700 non-sudden deaths, in about 49,000
cases (which is 56.5%!) the physicians made decisions that possi-
bly or actually shortened the patients' lives. This figure exceeds
all previous estimates.

As a consequence of the report of the governmental committee,
euthanasia will not be legalized in Holland. The government has
renounced the idea. Indeed, involuntary euthanasia turned out to
be an important part of the practice. Therefore, the new regulations on euthanasia approved by the Parliament in 1993,
acknowledge the practice of euthanasia but do not legalize it.
The article of the Penal Code which prohibits euthanasia has not
been abolished.

FEAR AND UNCERTAINTY

What is happening to the society which has embraced euthanasia? Of course, there is very much life and work as usual. You shouldn't imagine horrors seen in the streets of Dutch cities. It's not the case. If there is a danger, if there is a change, it is not apparent at the first glance. It takes some insight to perceive the future dangers even now. But change is there: In general, you can say that the message society sends to its members is changed now. Instead of, "everybody has the right to be around; we want to keep you with us, every one of you," the society that has accepted euthanasia tells people, "we wouldn't mind getting rid of you." And this message reaches not only the elderly and the sick, but all the weak and dependent. As a consequence, some groups live in fear and uncertainty. The Dutch Patients' Association stated in 1985, "The fear of euthanasia among people has considerably increased." Now the Association operates a hot-line for anxious patients and families, and this line is very busy every day...

EUTHANASIA IN THE U.S.

Hearing the news from Holland, people ask with apprehension whether euthanasia will come to the United States. But it has already come: by court orders unconscious persons are starved and dehydrated to death.

Heretofore, we used to admit that we were helpless at the bedside of a protractedly unconscious person, that we had no solution; there was none. The truth was that we could not do anything, we could only wait. We used to wait and shield the patient, trying to hope. Now it is claimed that there is a solution: when we destroy the patient, the problem ceases to exist.

We also used to acknowledge that, with very few exceptions, we did not know which unconscious patients might eventually recover. At present, verdicts of "irreversible coma" are pronounced with a certainty that admits no doubts. Hippocratic medicine's truthful, modest attitude has become obsolete. Instead, a new ethic is proclaimed, that of self-assured expediency.

13   EUTHANASIA IN THE NETHERLANDS

EUTHANASIA:
The Medicine of Mercy and Justice

Dutch Ministry of Justice

The following article, prepared by the Dutch Ministry of Justice, outlines the report for a commission inquiry into the medical practice with regard to euthanasia.

Points to Consider:

1. What definition of euthanasia is used by the Dutch Commission report?

2. What is implied by the statistics on cases of euthanasia death, and cases of doctors not complying with requests for euthanasia?

3. How can a doctor justify discontinuing treatment without an explicit request from the patient?

4. Why is aggressive treatment of pain not the answer to suffering?

Excerpted from a 1993 paper by the Netherland Ministry of Justice summarizing a report by the Commission set up by the Dutch government to inquire into medical practice with regard to euthanasia in the Netherlands.

Unbearable suffering and/or the natural desire to die peacefully were the only reason for doctors in the Netherlands to carry out euthanasia.

The commission of inquiry into medical practice with regard to euthanasia (Remmelink Commission) was set up by the Minister of Justice, Mr. E.M.H. Hirsch Ballin and the State Secretary of Welfare, Health and Cultural Affairs, Dr. J.H. Simons by a Ministerial Order of January 17, 1990. The Commission was chaired by Prof. J. Remmelink, Procurator-General at the Supreme Court of the Netherlands.

The assignment of the Commission was to report to the government on the state of affairs regarding the practice of action and inaction by a doctor that may lead to the end of a patient's life. The Commission and the researchers chose as their working definition the interpretation of the Government Commission on Euthanasia in its final report of 1985, that is to say: euthanasia is the deliberate termination of another's life at his request. The objective of this inquiry was also to acquire an overview of all potentially life-shortening medical decisions.

THE NATURE OF MEDICAL DECISIONS WITH REGARD TO THE END OF LIFE

From the research data the Commission concludes that nearly all the doctors in the Netherlands who are involved in patient care are faced with various medical decisions with regard to the end of life. Therefore these decisions belong to the normal field of activity of every doctor who is frequently confronted with deaths. The Commission stresses that decisions to carry out euthanasia make up only a fraction of all these decisions. General practitioners are frequently faced with requests for the termination of a life. That is why, in most cases, they are the ones who administer euthanasia. Least frequently euthanasia is carried out by doctors in nursing homes. However, the discontinuance of a life-prolonging treatment or not starting one, without an explicit request by the patient, occurs relatively often in nursing homes. For the most part these cases involve very old or demented patients, when in consultation with relatives and the nursing staff the decision is made not to treat (any longer) a fatal disorder, such as cardiac arrest or pneumonia. In these instances one can speak of "leaving nature to her own devices." This course of action is generally regarded to be good and proper exercise of a doctor's professional

Life-support system?

Cartoon by David Seavey. Copyright 1990, **USA Today**. Reprinted with permission.

duties. In foreign literature one comes across the assertion that in the Netherlands most cases of active termination of life occur in nursing homes. This assertion is contestable, as the research report shows.

EUTHANASIA (AND ASSISTANCE IN SUICIDE)

The data on the extent of euthanasia in the Netherlands, an extent that now has been determined scientifically (2,300 cases: 1.8 percent of all deaths, 130,000 a year), disprove certain ideas that circulate in society. (The same goes for the small number of cases of assistance in suicide; approximately 400.) This extent does not warrant the assumption that euthanasia in the Netherlands occurs on an excessive scale and that it is used increasingly as an alternative to good palliative or terminal care.

According to the Commission, the assumption mentioned above is not only disproved by the self-evident number of 2,300 cases a year, but also by the fact that doctors in the Netherlands are faced with about 9,000 requests for the termination of a patient's life. In other words: it happens more often that a doctor does not comply with a request for the termination of a life, for example, because he finds an alternative to euthanasia, than that he actually carries out euthanasia. The research results show that doctors feel strongly about the decision to accede to a patient's request for the termination of his life, and that they regard this decision not in the least as a convenient alternative to good terminal care. All in all the Commission sees no ground to suppose that this attitude is going to change in the future.

The Commission points out that there is no proof whatsoever in the research results for the suggestion made from time to time that lack of funds in the health sector were (or will become) a cause for the administration of euthanasia. Unbearable suffering and/or the natural desire to die peacefully were the only reason for doctors in the Netherlands to carry out euthanasia.

THE OMISSION OF LIFE-PROLONGING TREATMENT ON REQUEST

It is undisputed that a doctor may never commence a treatment without the patient's consent. Therefore, if the patient wants to abandon treatment or wants to discontinue a treatment already begun, the doctor will have to respect that wish, even if the patient's wish has been inspired by a longing for death. Situations such as these have no bearing at all on euthanasia. Perhaps unnecessarily the Commission wants to draw attention to the fact that what is at stake here is not the decision of a doctor, but that of a patient . . .

DELIBERATE LIFE-TERMINATING ACTIONS WITHOUT EXPLICIT REQUEST

The Commission first of all points out that active intervention by the doctor in those cases where there is no request at all, is usually inevitable because of the patient's death agony. That is why the Commission has labeled the action in question as care for the dying. The lack of a request for the termination of life under these circumstances only serves to make the decision process more difficult than in a situation in which there is indeed a sustained request, made freely and after careful consideration. The ultimate

86

justification for the intervention is in both cases the patient's unbearable suffering. So, medically speaking, there is little difference between these situations and euthanasia, because in both cases patients are involved who suffer terribly. The absence of a special request for the termination of life stems partly from the circumstance that the party in question is not (any longer) able to express his will because he is already in the terminal stage, and partly because of the demand for an explicit request is not in order when the treatment of pain and symptoms is intensified. The degrading condition the patient is in confronts the doctor.

According to the Commission, the intervention by the doctor can easily be regarded as an action that is justified by necessity, just like euthanasia. In a few dozen cases there were circumstances under which the doctor could have applied the procedure suitable for the decision process regarding the administration of euthanasia. According to the Commission, situations like these must be prevented in the future. One means to this end is strict compliance with the scrupulous care that is necessary when euthanasia is carried out, including the requirement that all facts of the case are put down in writing.

Finally the Commission remarks that the research report disproves the assertion often expressed, that non-voluntary active termination of life occurs more frequently in the Netherlands than voluntary termination.

THE OMISSION OF A LIFE-PROLONGING TREATMENT WITHOUT EXPLICIT REQUEST

Sometimes a doctor will discontinue a treatment or not commence one without an explicit request by the patient. After all, a doctor has the right to refrain from (further) treatment, if that treatment would be pointless according to objective medical standards. The Commission would define a treatment without any medical use as therapeutic interference that gives no hope whatsoever for any positive effect upon the patient. To the application of this kind of futile medicine, no one is entitled. It is undisputed that the decision whether a particular action is useful or not belongs to normal medical practice.

THE TREATMENT OF PAIN AND SYMPTOMS

The administration of medicine in order to treat pain or symptoms, is part of the normal duties of a doctor. The administration of these remedies in increasing doses may in certain cases have as a side effect a shortening of the patient's life. However, the alleviation of the patient's suffering remains the principal aim. The precipitation of death is not the intended result as such of the medical action. Thanks to the conscientious use of the available means for the treatment of pain or symptoms, the terminal phase of many incurable patients need no longer go hand in hand with prolonged and unbearable suffering.

The research shows nevertheless that pain killing alone does not suffice to make euthanasia redundant. First of all the Commission draws attention to the fact that this research also makes it clear that pain is not the most common motive for a request for the termination of life. The fear of total degeneration and the very natural wish to be able to pass away peacefully are just as important reasons to request the termination of one's life as pain is.

The doctors that were interviewed indicated that not all forms of pain can be treated successfully. Some pain can only be stopped by bringing and keeping the patient in a state of total unconsciousness. When confronted with that possibility, many patients ask for the termination of their life. From this information the Commission draws the conclusion that the opinion sometimes put forward, that more advanced techniques for the treatment of pain or symptoms would lead to fewer requests for euthanasia, is inaccurate...

THE LIMITS OF MEDICAL DUTY

Doctors see it as their prime responsibility to keep their patients alive. That is what their medical duty is primarily aimed at. If there is no possibility for recovery left, they still consider it their duty to alleviate the suffering and to give adequate care. There may come a moment when death has become inevitable and when the doctor, in view of a dignified end of life for his patient, must discontinue certain medical actions or never commence them at all, or, as part of the treatment of pain or symptoms, he may have to prescribe remedies that as a side effect might shorten the patient's life. In extreme cases there will be no other option left but active interference.

Especially doctors, but nurses as well, will have to be trained in terminal care. By terminal care the Commission means the whole of assistance and care on behalf of dying humans and their next of kin. Optimal care for someone who is dying implies that the doctor has knowledge of adequate treatments for pain, of alternatives for the treatment of complaints about unbearable pain and that he is aware of the moment when he must allow the process of dying to run its natural course. Doctors still lack sufficient knowledge of this care that also includes ethical and legal aspects. In a country that is rated among the best in the world when it comes to birth care, knowledge with regard to care for the dying should not be lacking.

14   EUTHANASIA IN THE NETHERLANDS

MERCY KILLING AND NEWBORNS:
An Overview

Matthew C. Vita

Matthew C. Vita wrote the following article for Cox News Service.

Points to Consider:

1. What is the stand of the Dutch Society for Voluntary Euthanasia on mercy killing of newborns?

2. Comment: "Sometimes care is helping a baby die."

3. What is the Dutch Pediatric Association proposing?

Matthew C. Vita, "Dutch Pediatricians Seek Extension of Accepted Euthanasia," **Cox News Service**, August 1992. Reprinted with permission.

Although euthanasia is technically illegal, the medical community estimates there are 2,300 mercy killings a year in Holland, a nation of 15 million.

Four months after the Dutch Parliament effectively decriminalized euthanasia for adults, pediatricians in Holland are seeking similar permission for the mercy killing of severely handicapped newborns.

Doctors in the Netherlands end the lives of about 10 newborns a year through lethal doses of medication, said Zier Versluys, who headed a Dutch Pediatric Association study of the issue.

"For these babies, life is a threat, not a perspective," Versluys said. "It's a very difficult thing to do, but sometimes care is helping a baby die."

Doctors routinely have disguised most of these cases — which involve only a fraction of the 200,000 births in Holland each year — as death by natural causes to avoid prosecution, even though charges rarely are brought. Now, a report from a panel of pediatricians led by Versluys is seeking "clear criteria" that — while not legalizing the mercy killing of newborns outright — would protect doctors from prosecution. The report, which will be debated by the Pediatric Association next month, recommends that guidelines similar to those governing euthanasia for adults be adopted for newborns.

The proposal has refocused attention on the euthanasia controversy in the Netherlands by bringing into the open what has until now been a less-publicized aspect of the debate. Euthanasia opponents have strongly criticized the report.

"There is no moral difference between killing a newborn baby or a mature person or someone who is at the end of his life," said Eimert van Middelkoop, a lawmaker from the religious Reformed Political Party. "In every case it is taking away someone's right to live."

Versluys said the country's 600 pediatricians are divided on the issue, which is one reason his panel was appointed.

Proponents of legalize euthanasia are holding back judgment. "We do not consider this as euthanasia because euthanasia is considered here in the Netherlands as a request for the termination of life," said Walter Nagel, secretary of the Dutch Society for

Voluntary Euthanasia, which boasts 60,000 members. "Newborns, of course, cannot make a request. So the term euthanasia is incorrect in this case."

Versluys said the majority of the infant euthanasia cases involve newborns with severe congenital malformations or with severe brain damage caused by oxygen deprivation before or at birth. He said his panel is proposing that the attending doctor decide whether to end a severely handicapped child's life, with the approval of its parents and the agreement of other physicians.

Although euthanasia is technically illegal, the medical community estimates there are 2,300 mercy killings a year in Holland, a nation of 15 million.

"If they are careful and follow instructions, the prosecutor will not prosecute them," said Liesbeth Rensman, a spokeswoman at the Dutch Ministry of Justice.

One doctor out of 600 who reported mercy killings last year was prosecuted, according to the Royal Dutch Medical Association.

In April, Parliament's second chamber effectively decriminalized the practice by adopting a set of guidelines for doctors to follow to avoid prosecution. The first chamber is scheduled to debate the question this fall and passage seems likely.

EUTHANASIA AND CHILDREN:
The Point

James P. Orlowski, Martin L. Smith & Jan Van Zwienen

Dr. James P. Orlowski, M.D., practices at the Department of Pediatrics and Adolescent Medicine, Section of Pediatric Critical Care, The Cleveland Clinic Foundation. Dr. Martin L. Smith, S.T.D., works at the Department of Ethics, the Cleveland Clinic Foundation, and Dr. Jan Van Zwienen, M.D., was a visiting international scholar in intensive care and research from the Netherlands at the Cleveland Clinic Foundation.

Points to Consider:

1. What does the term "nonvoluntary euthanasia" mean?

2. What is the incidence of newborn euthanasia in The Netherlands and in what cases is it practiced?

3. How can euthanasia for adolescent patients be viewed as an expanded application of voluntary active euthanasia?

4. What role do Dutch parents play in euthanasia of children under age seven?

5. How might acceptance of non-voluntary active euthanasia be viewed as "sliding down the slope"?

James P. Orlowski, M.D.; Martin L. Smith, S.T.D.; Jan Van Zwienen, M.D., "Pediatric Euthanasia," **American Journal of Diseases in Children (AJDC)**, Vol. 146, pp. 1440-46, December 1992. Copyright 1992, American Medical Association.

It is our judgment that pediatric active euthanasia, especially for infants and younger children who are not capable of participating in treatment decisions, is a distinctive and major step down "the slippery slope".

Pediatric euthanasia is currently practiced in the Netherlands on newborns, infants, children, and adolescents, although exact numbers are not known. Euthanasia in the Netherlands is generally assumed to be active and voluntary, but some cases of pediatric euthanasia would have to be characterized as nonvoluntary. Much of the motivation behind the euthanasia movement and the performance of pediatric euthanasia in the Netherlands is a genuine, compassionate desire to alleviate pain and suffering. In this study, we review the Dutch experience, with particular attention to the current practice of euthanasia on newborns, infants, children, and adolescents. We discuss pediatric euthanasia from an ethical point of view. We assert that more effective pain control, better symptom management, and psychosocial support of the dying and their families would alleviate the perception of suffering, and reduce the perceived need to resort to euthanasia.

It may come as a surprise to some that euthanasia is performed on newborns, infants, children, and adolescents as well as on adults in the Netherlands. The source of the surprise is twofold. First, because this aspect of the Dutch experience with euthanasia is rarely discussed in the literature. Second, because it is generally assumed that euthanasia, for reasons of safeguarding the participants, is practiced only on consenting and competent individuals who are fully cognizant of what is being requested and are capable of making an informed and unencumbered decision.

In this article, we examine the Dutch experience with euthanasia, in general, and then the specific aspects of pediatric euthanasia as gleaned from the Dutch medical literature and discussions with Dutch physicians.

DEFINITIONS AND DISTINCTIONS

Euthanasia, literally meaning "a good death", has come to refer to the act of painlessly putting to death persons suffering from incurable conditions or diseases. For the purpose of making distinctions, various qualifiers are regularly used with the word, although these qualifiers are not universally agreed to be appropriate.

Cartoon by Steve Sack. Reprinted with permission from the **Star Tribune**, Minneapolis.

Active euthanasia refers to the intentional termination of a life to relieve suffering, achieved by doing something. Passive euthanasia refers to death as a result of omitting or foregoing a life-preserving measure.

Voluntary euthanasia refers to the ending of the lives of persons at their informed request and free consent. Euthanasia can also be achieved without the consent of a person, which is termed nonvoluntary and includes infanticide and the killing of unconscious patients based on a surrogate's decision. Euthanasia against the will of the victim is termed involuntary.

Direct euthanasia occurs when life is ended actively and intentionally as the result of a specific action, whereas indirect euthanasia means allowing death to occur without a direct link between the action, intent, and result. The term indirect euthanasia is frequently used to describe the hastening of death by an action that is primarily intended to relieve suffering or promote some other good, but is also known to be potentially lethal, for example the use of morphine to alleviate air hunger and distress in a patient dying of respiratory failure.

Two additional terms that frequently arise in discussions on euthanasia are suicide (the killing of self) and assisted suicide (another person providing the means or assisting someone with self-killing).

THE DUTCH EXPERIENCE WITH EUTHANASIA

Euthanasia in the Netherlands is defined as "a deliberate life-ending action by another person than the concerned person at the enduring request of the latter" and "is, by necessity, voluntary." Using the above definitions and distinctions, what is generally termed euthanasia in the Netherlands is active, voluntary, direct euthanasia.

Euthanasia is illegal in the Netherlands, but through verbal agreements between the Justice Department and the Royal Dutch Medical Association, a physician will not be prosecuted if certain criteria are fulfilled. These include the following: the request or demand for euthanasia made of the patient's own free will and choice and not due to coercion (i.e., voluntary); the discussion of euthanasia in private to avoid covert or overt pressure; a document requesting euthanasia signed by the patient; reasons for euthanasia that do not include loneliness, depression, societal or family interests, or pain; time for the patient to think about the decision; and the opinion of other professionals who then concur with the physician's decision to proceed with euthanasia...

PEDIATRIC EUTHANASIA

Euthanasia of children occurs in the Netherlands even though the usual practice of euthanasia emphasizes that the patient must competently and voluntarily request it and must persist in this request.

The Dutch Pediatric Society surveyed the eight major neonatal centers in the country. Only four of the centers had written protocols for foregoing life-sustaining therapies in neonates. Five of the eight centers actively terminated the lives of neonates with a predicted poor quality of life, and three of the eight centers in certain circumstances openly terminated the life of older infants with severe birth defects. The Dutch Pediatric Society does not use the term euthanasia because in neonatology the patient is unable to ask for life-ending therapy.

Although exact numbers are not known, statements by the

THE CHILD WHO NEVER GREW

The innocent may not be killed and there is none more innocent than these children who never grow up. Were the right to kill any innocent person assumed by society, the effect would be monstrous. For first it might be only the helpless children who were killed, but then it might seem right to kill the helpless old. Euthanasia is a smooth sounding word, and it conceals its danger as smooth words do, but the danger is there, nonetheless.

Pearl S. Buck, "The Child Who Never Grew", **Reader's Digest**, September 1950: 25

Dutch Medical Association and Dutch Pediatric Society indicate that euthanasia is practiced in the Netherlands on infants and newborns. Personal communications with Dutch pediatricians also confirm that euthanasia of children is performed occasionally, involving patients with cancers, degenerative diseases, and chronic illnesses. It is less clear how many of these infant and childhood cases of euthanasia are active as opposed to passive. It is estimated that "300 handicapped newborn babies are intentionally allowed to die and the lives of 10 such babies are actively terminated each year" in the Netherlands. It is also claimed that a pediatric oncologist acknowledged that he supplied drugs to an average of six children under his care each year, sometimes without their parents' knowledge, to enable them to commit suicide whenever they "feel so inclined" ...

Conversations with pediatricians in the Netherlands suggest that the other major pediatric group undergoing euthanasia in the Netherlands is teenagers. The adolescent patients are usually those with cancer in the terminal stages of their disease and with a predicted life expectancy of only four to five days. The mode of death in many cases is actually assisted suicide rather than euthanasia. The teenager is prescribed a twice-lethal dose of pure, concentrated, phenobarbital powder that is self-administered by the patient at home. Sleep typically occurs approximately five minutes later and death shortly afterward.

One pediatric oncologist estimated that he used this technique about eight times per year. This physician saw approximately 160 new patients each year with 50 to 80 of them dying of their disease, for an incidence of euthanasia of approximately 10% in his specialty practice. This incidence of euthanasia of approximately 10% was consistent among the Dutch specialty physicians with whom we communicated. Conversations with pediatricians in the Netherlands suggest that assisted suicide is being employed more among teenagers because of unfavorable publicity surrounding the previous use of active euthanasia in this patient population. The physicians see assisted suicide as a less risky means of obtaining the same results. When assisted suicide is not possible, active euthanasia is employed.

In the Netherlands, the practice of pediatric euthanasia depends on age. If the child is younger than 16 years, the parents or guardians are consulted and involved in making the decision. If the parents or guardians refuse permission for euthanasia, the physician does not proceed. On the other hand, euthanasia generally is not performed if the child refuses, even if the parents request it. If the patient is between 16 and 18 years old, then parents or guardians are involved in the decision but do not have the right of veto over the patient's request for euthanasia.

Euthanasia of neonates and young children is in conflict with the standard practice of euthanasia being requested by the patient. It is obvious that infants cannot express a wish for euthanasia; so when it occurs in this patient population, it is appropriately labeled nonvoluntary. It is estimated by the Dutch Medical Association that although the lives of 300 newborns are ended in the Netherlands each year, it is only rarely by active killing. Many of these newborn children have severe handicaps and are allowed to die by withholding surgery or nutrition. The Remmelink Commission reported that 1399 newborns died in 1990 in the Netherlands, with half of them dying in the first week of life. The Commission gave no estimates of the number of deaths due to euthanasia, except to report that in a random sample, medication was administered to two of 35 infants with the express purpose of ending their lives. An additional four infants in the sample received medication for pain with the intended purpose of shortening their lives. In contrast, treatment was withheld or withdrawn from 12 of the 35 infants and no medical decisions concerning the end of life were made for the remaining 17 infants...

COMMENT

It is our judgment that pediatric active euthanasia, especially for

KILLING INFANTS

The line that 15 years ago I thought could be drawn at birth is turning out to be no line at all, and it has become clear that there is indeed a direct connection between the legalization of abortion and the legitimation of infanticide. For it is just as the great geneticist (and, from the other side, the opponents of abortion) insisted: if the objection to killing a fetus is removed, there will soon be no objection to killing a newborn infant.

Norman Podhoretz, "Sliding Down the Slope Toward Infanticide," **News America Syndicate**, 1982

infants and younger children who are not capable of participating in treatment decisions, is a distinctive and major step down "the slippery slope". The premise of the slippery slope argument is that a particular act, however innocuous, may yet lead to a host of similar but increasingly pernicious events. By moving from voluntary to nonvoluntary active euthanasia, a major slide down "the slope" has been made.

16 EUTHANASIA IN THE NETHERLANDS

EUTHANASIA AND CHILDREN:
The Counterpoint

Henk K.A. Visser, Hannie G.M. Aartsen, & Inez D. de Beaufort

Henk K. Visser, M.D., is affiliated with the Department of Pediatrics at the University Hospital in Rotterdam. Hannie G.M. Aartsen works with the Dutch Health Council. Inez D. de Beaufort works for the Department of Medical Ethics at Erasmus University in Rotterdam.

Points to Consider:

1. In the Netherlands, why is a high dosage of opioids not considered "indirect euthanasia"?

2. In general, what type of euthanasia is used with children in the Netherlands?

3. How did the "slippery slope" originate?

4. Considering the well-funded health care system in the Netherlands, what might be the incentive for pediatric euthanasia?

Henk K.A. Visser, M.D., Ph.D.; Hannie G.M. Aartsen, and Inez D. DeBeaufort, Ph.D., "Medical Decisions Concerning the End of Life in Children in the Netherlands," **American Journal of Diseases in Children (AJDC)**, Vol. 146, pp. 1429-31, December 1992. Copyright 1992, American Medical Association.

We do not agree that the Dutch find themselves on a slippery slope.

In this issue of *American Journal of Diseases in Children*, Orlowski et al discuss pediatric euthanasia in the Netherlands. We are disappointed about this article for several reasons. Orlowski et al have not reviewed, in a balanced way, the complex issue of euthanasia in adults and children. The authors seem to pretend otherwise, but in the Netherlands adult euthanasia and pediatric euthanasia are treated separately because of the fundamentally different medical, ethical, legal, and emotional grounds. Why did the authors not compare the discussions of pediatric euthanasia in the Netherlands with those in the United States? The article lacks factual accuracy. Furthermore, we do not agree with the two main conclusions of the authors, namely, that euthanasia is not needed if more effective pain control and psychological support for the dying are available and that the Dutch find themselves on a slippery slope.

We first point out some factual inaccuracies. Then, we briefly describe the current discussion in the Netherlands regarding pediatric euthanasia and end with a comment on the main conclusions of the authors. Although in the Netherlands the term euthanasia is used only for voluntary euthanasia, in this editorial we also use the term as defined by Orlowski et al...

PEDIATRIC EUTHANASIA

The authors state "practice of pediatric euthanasia depends on age" and mention age limits of 16 and 18 years. In practice, the ability of minors to express coherently their well-founded wishes is taken into account. The suggestion that fixed age limits exist is unfounded.

The article suggests that pediatric euthanasia, unlike voluntary euthanasia in adults, is rarely discussed in the Netherlands. In fact, there is a lot of discussion on both voluntary euthanasia in adults and nonvoluntary euthanasia in children. As previously mentioned, the subjects are considered to be separate problems because of the fundamentally different issues related to patient age.

The article suggests that physicians are pressured to perform pediatric euthanasia because of the threat of possible wrongful life suits. We think this particular pressure is over-emphasized. To our knowledge, no wrongful life or wrongful birth suit has been filed in the Netherlands.

One may gain a better insight into the ongoing discussions regarding pediatric euthanasia in the Netherlands by recognizing the important distinctions between various medical decisions concerning the end of life in infants and children.

ALLEVIATION OF PAIN AND/OR SYMPTOMS WITH HIGH DOSES OF OPIOIDS

One situation in which this decision may be made is that of a child who is in a terminal state of disseminated cancer with untreatable pain and suffering. The authors of the article describe this situation as "indirect euthanasia". In the Netherlands, euthanasia is not used to describe this kind of decision. Such a decision is regarded as part of normal medical treatment: the physician has the duty to alleviate the pain and suffering of patients and, in some situations, may feel responsible to further the process of dying using modern drugs available for pain relief.

In these situations, death occurs within a certain time, but death is not directly intended. There is a wide consensus in the Netherlands – and in the United States, we suppose – that such decisions can be morally and legally justified...

NONTREATMENT DECISIONS

Nontreatment decisions can be divided into two categories: (1) the decision not to start or prolong medical treatment because (further) treatment is evidently futile on medical grounds, and (2) the decision not to start or prolong treatment because (further) treatment is considered to be against the best interests of the child. The authors call both categories "passive euthanasia"...

When is stopping or continuing treatment in the best interests of the child? Which factors regarding the (future) quality of life should be taken into consideration, and how should they be weighed? (The Dutch Pediatric Society has not recommended a "scoring" system, but has published a report on criteria to be taken into account.) Who decides? Which procedures ought to be followed to guarantee a balanced and scrupulous decision-making process? All of these are complex issues that do not exclusively arise in the Netherlands, as the vast international literature shows.

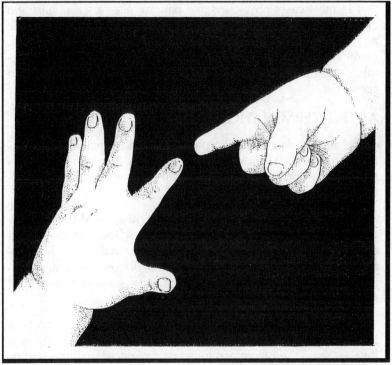

Illustration by Craig MacIntosh. Reprinted with permission from the **Star Tribune,** Minneapolis.

The current situation in the Netherlands is that the Dutch Pediatric Society and the Dutch Medical Association have published reports in which proposals for general guidelines and procedures are given. The Dutch Health Council is preparing a report on these problems. There has not yet been an open political debate in Parliament on these issues.

It is our impression that most will accept that stopping or foregoing treatment in certain cases under the procedural safeguards is ethically acceptable. From a legal point of view, this category is, and probably will remain, a problem because in these cases the decision not to treat or to stop treatment is guided by a complex of intentions. Therefore, any decision to prosecute will depend on the individual circumstances of each case.

Meanwhile, in the Netherlands, physicians and parents together make the decision, in concrete situations, acting in the best interests of the child. It is our strong impression and our experience that in most cases physicians and parents, after a scrupulous and careful decision-making process, reach a consensus. In the large pediatric departments and children's hospitals in the Netherlands, medical ethical committees evaluate such decisions and the carefulness of the procedures. The district public prosecutor is also consulted.

ACTIVE TERMINATION OF LIFE

The authors describe this type of decision as "active nonvoluntary euthanasia". This kind of decision may be made when nontreatment is not followed by death and untreatable pain and suffering continue.

The prevalence of active euthanasia in children in the Netherlands is, to our knowledge, extremely low. Orlowski and colleagues do not present new data, but refer in their article several times to personal communications or discussions with Dutch pediatricians. It is our experience that most cases of pediatric euthanasia involve nontreatment decisions.

On active nonvoluntary euthanasia in children there is no consensus in the Netherlands. For physicians, this type of decision is different from the beforementioned type of decision not to start or to forego medical treatment. Is there always a fundamental moral distinction between "active" and "passive" nonvoluntary pediatric euthanasia in the sense that passive euthanasia can never be justified? This seems to be the position of Orlowski and colleagues because they repeatedly express their concern regarding active pediatric euthanasia. Or is this distinction not always clear or morally decisive – the choice for death being the crucial issue, whether by passive or active means? There simply is no consensus...

MORE PALLIATIVE CARE AND PAIN CONTROL?

We strongly disagree with the authors that doctors in the Netherlands should receive more training in palliative care and pain control. Dutch pediatricians are well aware of modern techniques of pain control and take every effort, together with nurses, psychologists, child psychiatrists, and social workers, to improve the terminal care of their patients...

SLIPPERY SLOPE

The authors state that in their view pediatric active euthanasia in the Netherlands is a distinctive and major step down the slippery slope (the slope originating from the acceptance of active voluntary euthanasia). It is unclear how the authors judge passive pediatric euthanasia in relation to a slippery slope.

The slippery slope argument has different versions. Generally a logical (conceptual) and an empirical (psychological) version are distinguished.

The logical version is as follows: because of vague conceptual distinctions, one will be logically forced, if one accepts X (eg, voluntary active euthanasia), to accept Y (nonvoluntary euthanasia), although one holds the latter to be morally unacceptable. This is a reason not to accept X.

The empirical version states that accepting X will sooner or later lead to accepting Y because gradually an erosion of moral values would take place. With regard to the slippery slope argument, we make the following remarks:

(1) In our view, the dangers of a slippery slope with regard to pediatric euthanasia are not more (or less) real in the Netherlands than they are elsewhere. Physicians and parents will continue to face complex decisions regarding the end of life of seriously ill and handicapped children. Whether or not society accepts active voluntary euthanasia, the problems of decisions regarding the end of life of children will not be solved because children's situations differ fundamentally from those of competent adults for whom euthanasia is considered. The logical version, in our view, is not very convincing because the concept of voluntary euthanasia in itself is not vague and does not logically force someone who accepts voluntary euthanasia to accept nonvoluntary euthanasia.

(2) Facing decisions regarding the end of life of children, one should always be aware of, though not paralyzed by, the dangers of a slippery slope. This holds, in our view, for both active and passive pediatric euthanasia. To focus one's worries on active pediatric euthanasia is under-estimating the moral complexity of nontreatment decisions. Acknowledging the existence of these problems, encouraging public debate, and scrupulously evaluating the ethical and legal considerations of these decisions are of the utmost importance in preventing a slippery slope.

(3) For those who hold that both active and passive forms of pediatric euthanasia are always morally unjustified, it is "too late"

for other-minded people who do not exclude the possibility that passive or active pediatric euthanasia can sometimes be justified. Any other point of view is in itself considered a slippery slope. Those holding such stalwart opinions have apparently solved the issues of what to do when confronted with a severely handicapped and suffering child. We have to admit that we have not solved those issues.

(4) For those who, in the context of the slippery slope argument, draw the line between passive and active pediatric euthanasia, two significant questions remain: Is such a distinction sufficiently clear and morally decisive? Why would a moral justification of passive pediatric euthanasia not lead to a slippery slope?

(5) To prove that a slippery slope has occurred in one country (and not in another) one needs figures to show that in fact the situation at a certain time after the acceptance of a certain policy (e.g., the acceptance of voluntary euthanasia) was worse than it was before. No such data are available.

As a last remark, we strongly disagree with the suggestion that motivations for pediatric euthanasia could be "a desire to conserve societal resources for those with better prognoses, and desire to alleviate family and care-giver distress." The only motivation is the individual patient's best interests. In the well-funded health care system in the Netherlands, there is no incentive for hospitals or nursing homes to have patients die soon. Moreover, in the Netherlands, all facilities are available for the care of severely handicapped children.

VALUES IN CONFLICT

Terminating Life

In a landmark 1976 case, Karen Ann Quinlan's parents won the right to have their comatose daughter's respirator unplugged. They believed it prolonged her suffering. She did not die as expected and a new issue arose involving comatose and terminally ill patients. Should feeding tubes, for example, be disconnected when there is no hope for recovery. Examine the statements and ideas in conflict below and evaluate and discuss them as indicated.

Guidelines

Good readers make clear distinctions between descriptive articles that relate factual information and articles that express a point of view. Articles that express editorial commentary and analysis are featured in this publication. Examine the following statements. Then try to decide if any of these statements take a similar position to any of the authors in Chapter Three. Working as individuals or in small groups, try to match the point of view in each statement below with the most appropriate reading number in front of each statement. Mark (O) for any statement that cannot be associated with the point of view of any opinion in Chapter Three.

_____1. Feeding tubes should be removed from comatose patients with no hope for recovery.

_____2. Feeding tubes should never be removed from comatose patients. All patients have a right to food and water, the basic elements of life.

_____3. Close relatives should decide when medical treatment should be withdrawn when there is no clear indication of a patient's wishes.

_____4. Relatives should not be given control over life and death situations in the absence of a living will that clearly indicates a patient's wishes.

_____ 5. Any decision to stop feeding a patient would enhance death, not life. It would be one step closer to euthanasia.

_____ 6. Denying food and water to a terminally ill patient is murder.

_____ 7. Denying food and water to a terminally ill patient is not murder if a living will indicates that is what the patient desires.

_____ 8. Providing food and water is not sophisticated medical treatment. It is every patient's need, and medical practitioners have a moral obligation to provide it.

_____ 9. It is ethical to withhold all means of medical treatment, including food and water, from persons in irreversible comas.

_____10. It is time to recognize that the most important right of people unable to speak for themselves is the right to be cared for and not to be killed.

CHAPTER 4

PHYSICIAN-ASSISTED SUICIDE:
IDEAS IN CONFLICT

17 PHYSICIAN-ASSISTED SUICIDE: IDEAS IN CONFLICT

ASSISTED SUICIDE MEANS DEATH WITH DIGNITY

Timothy E. Quill, M.D.

Timothy E. Quill, M.D., is a practicing physician at the Genesee Hospital in Rochester, New York. The following article appeared in The New England Journal of Medicine.

Points to Consider:

1. What is the philosophy of "comfort care"?

2. Briefly explain what Dr. Quill meant by exploring boundaries: spiritual, legal, professional, and personal.

3. Why did Dr. Quill give as cause of death "acute leukemia"?

4. What two conditions does Dr. Quill put on the "range of help" he can provide?

Abstracted from information appearing in **NEJM**, Timothy E. Quill, M.D., "Death and Dignity: A Case of Individualized Decision-Making," **The New England Journal of Medicine,** Vol. 324, pp. 691-94, March 7, 1991.

Although I did not assist her in suicide directly, I helped indirectly to make it possible, successful, and relatively painless.

Diane was feeling tired and had a rash. A common scenario, though there was something subliminally worrisome that prompted me to check her blood count...Through much of her adult life, she had struggled with depression and alcoholism. I had come to know, respect, and admire her over the previous eight years as she confronted these problems and gradually overcame them.

Not surprisingly, the repeated blood count was abnormal, and detailed examination of the peripheral blood smear showed myelocytes. I advised her to come into the hospital, explaining that we needed to do a bone marrow biopsy and make some decisions relatively rapidly. She came to the hospital knowing what we would find. She was terrified, angry, and sad. Although we knew the odds, we both clung to the thread of possibility that it might be something else.

The bone marrow confirmed the worst: acute myelomonocytic leukemia...Our oncologist broke the news to Diane and began making plans to insert a Hickman catheter and begin induction chemotherapy that afternoon. When I saw her shortly thereafter, she was enraged at his presumption that she would want treatment, and devastated by the finality of the diagnosis. All she wanted to do was go home and be with her family. She had no further questions about treatment and in fact had decided that she wanted none...

I have been a longtime advocate of active, informed patient choice of treatment or nontreatment, and of a patient's right to die with as much control and dignity as possible. Yet there was something about her giving up a 25 percent chance of long-term survival in favor of almost certain death that disturbed me. I had seen Diane fight and use her considerable inner resources to overcome alcoholism and depression, and I half expected her to change her mind over the next week...

ANOTHER AREA

Just as I was adjusting to her decision, she opened up another area that would stretch me profoundly. It was extraordinarily important to Diane to maintain control of herself and her own dignity during the time remaining to her. When this was no longer

111

possible, she clearly wanted to die. As a former director of a hospice program, I know how to use pain medicines to keep patients comfortable and lessen suffering. I explained the philosophy of comfort care, which I strongly believe in. Although Diane understood and appreciated this, she had known of people lingering in what was called relative comfort, and she wanted no part of it. When the time came, she wanted to take her life in the least painful way possible. Knowing of her desire for independence and her decision to stay in control, I thought this request made perfect sense. I acknowledged and explored this wish but also thought that it was out of the realm of currently accepted medical practice and that it was more than I could offer or promise. In our discussion, it became clear that preoccupation with her fear of a lingering death would interfere with Diane's getting the most out of the time she had left until she found a safe way to ensure her death. I feared the effects of a violent death on her family, the consequences of an ineffective suicide that would leave her lingering in precisely the state she dreaded so much, and the possibility that a family member would be forced to assist her, with all the legal and personal repercussions that would follow. She discussed this at length with her family. They believed that they should respect her choice. With this in mind, I told Diane that information was available from the Hemlock Society that might be helpful to her.

SUICIDE

A week later she phoned me with a request for barbiturates for sleep. Since I knew that this was an essential ingredient in a Hemlock Society suicide, I asked her to come to the office to talk things over. She was more than willing to protect me by participating in a superficial conversation about her insomnia, but it was important to me to know how she planned to use the drugs and to be sure that she was not in despair or overwhelmed in a way that might color her judgment. In our discussion, it was apparent that she was having trouble sleeping, but it was also evident that the security of having enough barbiturates available to commit suicide when and if the time came would leave her secure enough to live fully and concentrate on the present. It was clear that she was not despondent and that in fact she was making deep, personal connections with her family and close friends. I made sure that she knew how to use the barbiturates for sleep, and also that she knew the amount needed to commit suicide. We agreed to meet regularly, and she promised to meet with me before taking

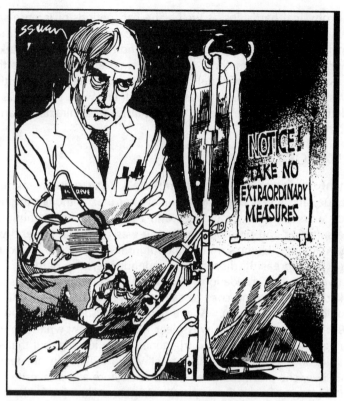

Cartoon by David Seavey. Copyright 1988, **USA Today**. Reprinted with permission.

her life, to ensure that all other avenues had been exhausted. I wrote the prescription with an uneasy feeling about the boundaries I was exploring — spiritual, legal, professional, and personal. Yet I also felt strongly that I was setting her free to get the most out of the time she had left, and to maintain dignity and control on her own terms until her death.

The next several months were very intense and important for Diane. Her son stayed home from college, and they were able to be with one another and say much that had not been said earlier. Her husband did his work at home so that he and Diane could spend more time together. She spent time with her closest friends. I had her come into the hospital for a conference with our residents, at which she illustrated in a most profound and personal way the importance of informed decision making, the right to refuse treatment, and the extraordinarily personal effects of illness and interaction with the medical system. There were emotional and physical hardships as well. She had periods of intense sadness and anger. Several times she became very weak, but she received transfusions as an outpatient and responded with marked improvement of symptoms. She had two serious infections that responded surprisingly well to empirical courses of oral antibiotics. After three tumultuous months, there were two weeks of relative calm and well-being, and fantasies of a miracle began to surface.

FINAL GOODBYES

Unfortunately, we had no miracle. Bone pain, weakness, fatigue, and fevers began to dominate her life. Although the hospice workers, family members, and I tried our best to minimize the suffering and promote comfort, it was clear that the end was approaching. Diane's immediate future held what she feared the most — increasing discomfort, dependence, and hard choices between pain and sedation. She called up her closest friends and asked them to come over to say goodbye, telling them that she would be leaving soon. As we had agreed, she let me know as well. When we met, it was clear that she knew what she was doing, that she was sad and frightened to be leaving, but that she would be even more terrified to stay and suffer. In our tearful goodbye, she promised a reunion in the future at her favorite spot on the edge of Lake Geneva, with dragons swimming in the sunset.

Two days later her husband called to say that Diane had died. She had said her final goodbyes to her husband and son that morning, and asked them to leave her alone for an hour. After an hour, which must have seemed an eternity, they found her on the couch, lying very still and covered by her favorite shawl. There was no sign of struggle. She seemed to be at peace. They called me for advice about how to proceed. When I arrived at their house, Diane indeed seemed peaceful. Her husband and son were quiet. We talked about what a remarkable person she had been. They seemed to have no doubts about the course she had chosen or about their cooperation, although the unfairness of her illness and the finality of her death were overwhelming to us all.

I called the medical examiner to inform him that a hospice patient had died. When asked about the cause of death, I said, "Acute leukemia." He said that was fine and that we should call a funeral director. Although acute leukemia was the truth, it was not the whole story. Yet any mention of suicide would have given rise to a police investigation and probably brought the arrival of an ambulance crew for resuscitation. Diane would have become a "coroner's case", and the decision to perform an autopsy would have been made at the discretion of the medical examiner. The family or I could have been subject to criminal prosecution, and I to professional review, for our roles in support of Diane's choices. Although I truly believe that the family and I gave her the best care possible, allowing her to define her limits and directions as much as possible, I am not sure the law, society, or the medical profession would agree. So I said "acute leukemia" to protect all of us, to protect Diane from an invasion into her past and her body, and to continue to shield society from the knowledge of the degree of suffering that people often undergo in the process of dying. Suffering can be lessened to some extent, but in no way eliminated or made benign, by the careful intervention of a competent, caring physician, given current social constraints.

CONCLUSION

Diane taught me about the range of help I can provide if I know people well and if I allow them to say what they really want. She taught me about life, death, and honesty and about taking charge and facing tragedy squarely when it strikes. She taught me that I can take small risks for people that I really know and care about. Although I did not assist her in suicide directly, I helped indirectly to make it possible, successful, and relatively painless. Although I know we have measures to help control pain and lessen suffering, to think that people do not suffer in the process of dying is an illusion. Prolonged dying can occasionally be peaceful, but more often the role of the physician and family is limited to lessening but not eliminating severe suffering.

I wonder how many families and physicians secretly help patients over the edge into death in the face of such severe suffering. I wonder how many severely ill or dying patients secretly take their lives, dying alone in despair. I wonder whether the image of Diane's final aloneness will persist in the minds of her family, or if they will remember more the intense, meaningful months they had together before she died. I wonder whether Diane struggled in that last hour, and whether the Hemlock Society's way of death by suicide is the most benign. I wonder why Diane, who gave so much to so many of us, had to be alone for the last hour of her life. I wonder whether I will see Diane again, on the shore of Lake Geneva at sunset, with dragons swimming on the horizon.

18   PHYSICIAN-ASSISTED SUICIDE: IDEAS IN CONFLICT

THE DANGERS OF LEGALIZING PHYSICIAN-ASSISTED SUICIDE

Herbert Hendin, M.D., and Gerald Klerman, M.D.

Herbert Hendin, M.D., and Gerald Klerman, M.D., examine physician-assisted suicide in the light of what is known about suicide and terminal illness, exploring the potential for abuse if legalization occurs. The elderly, those frightened by illness, and the depressed of all ages could be potential victims.

Points to Consider:

1. Comment: "Patients who desire an early death during a terminal illness are usually suffering from a treatable mental illness."

2. How might psychiatric evaluation make the difference between choosing life and choosing death?

3. How can depression coexisting with serious illness be treated?

4. Who might be particularly vulnerable if physician-assisted suicide were legalized?

Herbert Hendin, M.D., and Gerald Klerman, M.D., "Physician-Assisted Suicide: The Dangers of Legalization," **American Journal of Psychiatry**, January 1993. © 1993, American Psychiatric Association. Reprinted with permission.

This is not an evaluation that can be made by the average physician unless he or she has had extensive experience with depression and suicide.

There are situations when helping a terminally ill patient end his or her life seems appropriate. For centuries physicians have helped such patients die. Why should we not protect them and at the same time make it easier for the terminally ill to end their lives by legalizing physician-assisted suicide? The movement to do so represents such a drastic departure from established social policy and medical tradition that it needs to be evaluated in the light of what we now know about suicide and terminal illness.

We know that 95% of those who kill themselves have been shown to have a diagnosable psychiatric illness in the months preceding suicide.[1-4] The majority suffer from depression, which can be treated. This is particularly true of the elderly, who are more prone than younger victims to take their lives during the type of acute depressive episode that responds most effectively to modern available treatments.[3] Other diagnoses among the suicides include alcoholism, substance abuse, schizophrenia, and panic disorder; treatments are available for all of these illnesses.

Advocates of physician-assisted suicide try to convey the impression that in terminally ill patients the wish to die is totally different from suicidal intent in those without terminal illness. However, like other suicidal individuals, patients who desire an early death during a terminal illness are usually suffering from a treatable mental illness, most commonly a depressive condition.[5] Strikingly, the overwhelming majority of the terminally ill fight for life to the end. Some may voice suicidal thoughts in response to transient depression or severe pain, but these patients usually respond well to treatment for depressive illness and pain medication and are grateful to be alive.

STUDIES

Studies of those who have died by suicide have pointed out the nonrational elements of the wish to die in reaction to serious illness. More individuals, particularly elderly individuals, killed themselves because they feared or mistakenly believed they had cancer than killed themselves and actually had cancer.[6, 7] In the same vein, preoccupation with suicide is greater in those awaiting the results of tests for HIV antibodies than in those who know that

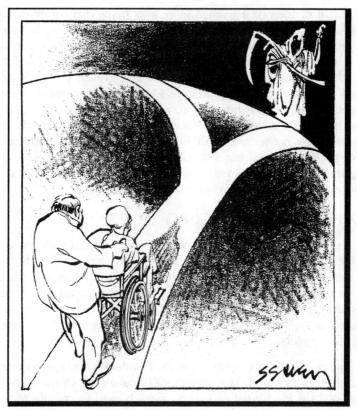

Cartoon by David Seavey. Copyright 1990, **USA Today**. Reprinted with permission.

they are HIV positive.[8]

Given the advances in our medical knowledge and treatment ability, a thorough psychiatric evaluation for the presence of a treatable disorder may literally make the difference between choosing life or choosing death for patients who express the wish to die or to have assisted suicide. This is not an evaluation that can be made by the average physician unless he or she has had extensive experience with depression and suicide.[9]

Even the highly publicized cases that have been put forward by the advocates of legalizing assisted suicide dramatize the dangers and abuses we would face when those who are not qualified to do so evaluate such patients or when we accept at face value a patient's assertion that he or she prefers death. Perhaps the first such case was featured in a front-page story more than a decade ago.[10] It concerned a woman who, after being diagnosed as having breast cancer, brought together her friends and her husband (who was a psychologist), filmed her farewells, and took a lethal overdose. For years the woman had been an advocate of the "right to suicide". Her film became a television documentary, and media stories portrayed her as something of a pioneer. A pioneer for what? Does her story contain a message we wish to send to the thousands of women facing possible breast surgery? The woman was not terminally ill; her cancer was operable. Although her psychologist husband supported her decision and felt it was appropriate, surely he was not the person to evaluate her. Was her choice as rational as everyone claimed?...

DEPRESSION AND ANXIETY

Depression, which is often covert and can coexist with physical illness, is, together with anxiety and the wish to die, often the first reaction to the knowledge of serious illness and possible death. This demoralizing triad can usually be treated by a combination of empathy, psychotherapy, and medication. The decision whether or not to live with illness is likely to be different with such treatment.

The publications of groups like the Hemlock Society, who advocate a more general "right to suicide", make clear that physician-assisted suicide for patients who have less than six months to live (as in the recently defeated California and State of Washington proposals) is but a first step in their campaign. Only a small percentage of the people they are trying to reach are terminally ill. The terminally ill, in fact, constitute only a small portion (less than 3%) of the total number of suicides.[1, 3, 9] Right-to-suicide groups have been joined in their efforts by well-meaning physicians concerned with the plight of the terminally ill.

Discussions of the right to suicide or the rationality of suicide in particular cases have tended to ignore the potential for abuse were physician-assisted suicide to be legalized. Particularly vulnerable potential victims would be the elderly, those frightened by illness, and the depressed of all ages.

The elderly are often made to feel that their families would prefer that they were gone. Societal sanction for physician-assisted suicide for the terminally ill is likely to encourage family members so inclined to pressure the infirm and the elderly and to collude with uninformed or unscrupulous physicians to provide such

---

NEVER-ENDING QUEST

Medicine, and the mindset that supports its never-ending quest for "a cure", must realize that its own hubris has contributed to the loss of trust among patients and would-be patients — ultimately, all of us. Medicine must both acknowledge and teach us its limits in staving off for a time our natural end, our own mortality. Though it must, like all of us, finally bow to death, medicine must never directly assist our dying.

"Not Before Time," **Commonweal**, October 11, 1991

---

deaths. Some advocates of changing social and medical policy toward suicide concede that such abuses are likely to occur but feel that this is a price we should be willing to pay.[13]

WILLING VICTIMS

Those whose terror of illness persuades them that quick death is the best solution may be willing victims of physicians who advocate assisted suicide. A woman in the early stages of Alzheimer's who was fearful of the progress of the disease was seen briefly by Dr. Jack Kevorkian, a retired pathologist in Michigan with a passionate commitment to promoting assisted suicide and the use of his "suicide machine". After a brief contact he decided she was a suitable candidate. He used the machine to help her kill herself. Is he the person who should be making such a determination? No Michigan law prohibits assisted suicide (19 states do not have such laws), but Dr. Kevorkian was admonished by the court not to engage in the practice again. Disregarding the admonition, he subsequently provided machines to two more women who were seriously but not terminally ill.[14] They used the machines to kill themselves. Dr. Kevorkian's license to practice medicine has since been "summarily suspended," but a Michigan judge ruled that he could not be prosecuted for murder in the absence of a state law prohibiting assisting a suicide.

Societal sanction for physician-assisted suicide is likely to encourage assisted suicide by nonphysicians, rendering those who are depressed, with or without physical illness, vulnerable to exploitation. Such abuse already exists. For example, a young man gave a depressed young woman he knew a lethal quantity of sleeping pills. He sat with her and fed them to her as she ate ice cream. While she was doing so, he persuaded her that, since she was going to die, she should write out a will leaving him her possessions. He went home and told his roommate what he had done; the roommate called the police and the young woman was saved. The young man went unpunished because he did what he did in a state with no law prohibiting assisted suicide.[11]

SUICIDE PACTS

So-called suicide pacts, often romanticized by the press, provide another example of such abuse. Published case reports confirm our own clinical experience, which indicates that such pacts are usually instances where a man who wishes to end his life coerces a woman into joining him as proof of her love.[11, 15,16] In her book, her taped suicide note, her letters, and conversations with friends, the former wife of Derek Humphry, the founder of the Hemlock Society, made clear that she was tormented by having actively participated with Humphry in the suicide pact of her parents. Although her 92-year-old father may have been ready to die, she was aware that her 78-year-old mother was not.[17-19]

Surely there is a price to be paid for current policy where physicians, patients, and family members must act secretly or may be unwilling to act even in situations where it seems appropriate. The protection of the honorable physician does not now warrant legalizing physician-assisted suicide in a society where the public is relatively uninformed of present abuses involving assisted suicide and the potential for much greater abuses if legalization occurs. It took us several decades to become knowledgeable about when it may be appropriate to withdraw life support systems. We are not close to that point with physician-assisted suicide.

PSYCHIATRIC EVALUATION

Nor by itself can evaluation of the patient by psychiatrists knowledgeable about suicide, depression, and terminal illness provide us with a simple solution to a complex social problem. Certainly, the individual physician confronted with someone requesting assisted suicide should seek such consultation. There is still too much we do not know about such patients, too much study yet to be done before we could mandate psychiatric evaluation for such patients and define conditions under which assisted suicide would be legal. We are likely to find that those who seek to die in the last days of terminal illness are a quite different population from those whose first response to the knowledge of serious illness is to turn to suicide.

Not all problems are best resolved by a statute. We do not convict or prosecute every case in which someone assists in a suicide, even in states where it is illegal. Given the potential for abuse, however, to give assisted suicide legal sanction is to give a dangerous license.

In some cultures (the Alorese are perhaps the most famous example), when people became seriously ill, they took to their beds, stopped eating, and waited to die. How we deal with illness, age, and decline says a great deal about who and what we are, both as individuals and as a society. The growing number of people living to old age and the increasing incidence of depression in people of all ages present us with a medical challenge. Our efforts should concentrate on providing treatment, relieving pain for the intractably ill, and, in the case of terminal illness, helping the individual come to terms with death.

If those advocating legalization of assisted suicide prevail, it will be a reflection that as a culture we are turning away from efforts to improve our care of the mentally ill, the infirm, and the elderly. Instead, we would be licensing the right to abuse and exploit the fears of the ill and depressed. We would be accepting the view of those who are depressed and suicidal that death is the preferred solution to the problems of illness, age, and depression.

REFERENCES

1 Robins E, Murphy G, Wilkenson RH Jr, Gassner S, Kayes J: Some clinical considerations in the prevention of suicide based on a study of 134 successful suicides. Am J Public Health 1959; 49:888-899

2 Dorpat TL, Ripley HS: A study of suicide in the Seattle area. Compr Psychiatry 1960; 1:349-359

3 Barraclough B, Bunch J, Nelson B, Sainsbury P: A hundred cases of suicide: clinical aspects. Br J Psychiatry 1974; 125:355-373

4 Rich DC, Young D,Fowler, RC: San Diego Suicide Study, I: young vs old subjects. Arch Gen Psychiatry 1986; 43-577-582

5 Brown JH, Henteleff P, Barakat S, Rowe CJ: Is it normal for terminally ill patients to desire death? Am J Psychiatry 1986; 143:208-211

6 Conwell Y, Caine ED, Olsen K: Suicide and cancer in later life. Hosp Community Psychiatry 1990; 41:1334-1339

7 Dorpat TL, Anderson WF, Ripley HS: The relationship of physical illness to suicide, in Suicidal Behaviors: Diagnosis and Management. Edited by Resnick HLP. Boston, Little, Brown, 1968

8 Perry S: Suicidal ideation and HIV testing. JAMA 1990; 263:679-682

9 Conwell Y, Caine ED:Rational suicide and the right to die: reality and myth. N Engl J Med 1991; 15:1100-1103

10Johnston L: Artist ends her life after ritual citing "self-termination" right. New York Times, June 17, 1979, p A1

11Hendin H: Suicide in America. New York, WW Norton, 1982

12Quill TE: Death and dignity — a case of individualized decision making. N Engl J Med 1991; 324:691-694

13Batten MP: Manipulated suicide, in Suicide: The Philosophical Issues. Edited by Batten M, May D. New York, St Martins Press, 1980

14Doctor in suicides assails US ethics. New York Times, Nov 3 1991, p A1

15Noyes R, Frye S, Hartford C: Single case study: conjugal suicide pact. J Nerv Ment Dis 1977; 165:72-75

16Mehta D, Mathew P, Mehta S: Suicide pact in a depressed elderly couple: case report. J Am Geriatr Soc 1978; 26:136-158

17Wickett A: Double Exit. Eugene, Ore, Hemlock Society, 1989

18Gabriel T: A fight to the death. New York Times Magazine, Dec 8, 1991, p 46

19Abrams G: A bitter legacy — angry accusations abound after the suicide of Hemlock Society co-founder Ann Humphry. Los Angeles Times, View section, p 1

19 PHYSICIAN-ASSISTED SUICIDE: IDEAS IN CONFLICT

THE ARGUMENT FOR ACTIVE VOLUNTARY EUTHANASIA

Howard Brody

Howard Brody, M.D., wrote the following article which appeared in The New England Journal of Medicine.

Points to Consider:

1. Why do the issues of abortion and assisted death need adjudication rather than resolution?

2. Discuss: "Denying that medicine can do anything to help in the patient's plight is an abrogation of medical power."

3. Why is it preferable for the patient to have the means to end life?

4. Briefly summarize the function of the review panel and the intra-professional review.

Excerpted from information appearing in **NEJM**, Howard Brody, M.D., Ph.D., "Assisted Death — A Compassionate Response to Medical Failure," **The New England Journal of Medicine**, Vol. 327, pp. 1384-88, November 5, 1992.

I have argued that we do not want an absolute prohibition against physician-assisted death.

Is it ever morally appropriate for physicians to assist a patient's dying, either by providing the means or by directly causing death? What should be the stance of the law toward physician-assisted death?

We have usually tried to resolve these questions through appeals to ethical rights, duties, and consequences. This search for a resolution has proved unsatisfactory. In the most difficult and compelling cases, the ethical rights, duties, and consequences seem fairly evenly balanced on both sides of the argument. Any resolution in terms of standard moral principles seems to reject the important moral considerations on one side or the other. One may affirm a physician's basic commitment to the preservation of life, but only at the cost of denying the weight of the physician's duty to relieve suffering and to respect the patient's thoughtful choices – or vice versa. In this regard, the debate over assisted death shares important features with the debate over abortion.

The philosopher Hilary Putnam, using abortion as an example, claimed that what we need in such situations is not resolution but adjudication. We cannot resolve these moral tensions by making one side of the tension disappear. Instead, we must learn to live with these tensions with a pluralistic society. This requires more reliance on negotiation, compromise, and practical reasoning, and less on abstract ethical theory ...

By assisted death I mean either voluntary, active euthanasia, as now commonly practiced in the Netherlands and as proposed in an unsuccessful referendum in Washington State in 1991, or assisted suicide, in which the patient is provided at his or her request with sufficient medication or other means to end life, with the knowledge that the patient intends to use the medication for that purpose. (In my view the "suicide machine" of Dr. Jack Kevorkian falls somewhere between these two practices but is nevertheless included under the general heading of assisted death.)

The call for the right to a physician's assistance in dying (urged by 55 to 65 percent of the U.S. public in all available opinion polls) seems based in large part on the fear that physicians will not in general see a good death as a success story and will fail to use available medical skills toward that end. People fear that physi-

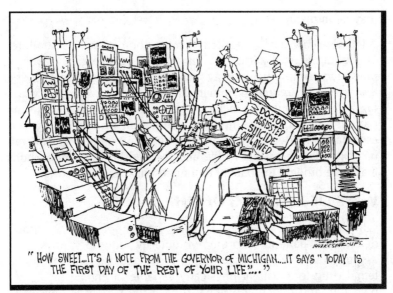

" HOW SWEET...IT'S A NOTE FROM THE GOVERNOR OF MICHIGAN....IT SAYS " TODAY IS THE FIRST DAY OF THE REST OF YOUR LIFE "..."

Bill Schorr, reprinted by permission of UFS, Inc.

cians will either overtreat them with life-prolonging technology long after a return of meaningful function is impossible or abandon them when they need control of symptoms and emotional support. It is moral cowardice and social unresponsiveness on the part of the medical profession not to state in the strongest possible terms that either overtreatment or abandonment in these circumstances is inappropriate care. Therefore, a good death as a medical success story proclaims a standard that, if it had the confidence of the public, would presumably reduce the demand for assisted death by a substantial degree.

Still, physicians do not have the luxury of simply describing the optimal outcome; we also have to plan what to do when things do not go well. A few patients will face a bad death despite all medical efforts. This may arise for at least three reasons, which the public must understand, lest unrealistic expectations of medical miracles become even more inflated. First, the ravages of disease may simply thwart all medical efforts to prolong life to the natural span or to restore useful and dignified function. Second, medical interventions may succeed only partially, extending life but leaving the patient lacking in some important element of function and dignity. Third, in a small percentage of cases palliative efforts will fail; for example, pain may persist despite full and appropriately timed doses of narcotics, or the toxic effect of the palliative agents may be intolerable.

In these few cases, physicians must confront medical failure. The failure is not by itself blameworthy or negligent. But what if physicians simply walk away from the failure, perhaps cloaking themselves in arguments from tradition? I wish to argue that walking away, denying that medicine can do anything to help in the patient's plight, is an immortal abrogation of medical power, especially in cases in which the prior exercise of the medical craft has extended the patient's life and resulted in the complications that have brought the patient to the present state of suffering...

WAYS OF ASSISTING DEATH

In the exceptional case in which we cannot achieve a good death for a patient, who then voluntarily requests a physician-assisted death, two practices might prove defensible: providing a lethal drug to a patient physically capable of ending his or her own life, and injecting a lethal drug if the patient is physically incapable of causing death.

The first is preferred over the second for reasons stressed by Quill but sometimes lost sight of. It is not preferable because the physician is less directly involved as a casual agent; letting the patient do the dirty work can be an abrogation of responsibility rather than an exercise in professional integrity. Instead, the preference lies in the potentially therapeutic effect of both having the means to end one's life and having personal control over the time and setting of their use. Quill contends that Diane may have gained several months of happy and functional life because of the reassurance provided by her bottle of barbiturates, which she would have been denied had he failed to prescribe them. Had Diane eventually died comfortably and at peace because she had the pills, but without actually using them, her death would have been a good death rather than a medical failure. (Indeed, this may be the most salient counterargument against my main point, that assisted death ought to be seen as a last resort.)

There are psychological reasons to prefer patient control over physician-administered lethal injection whenever possible. The normal human response to facing the final moment before death, when one has control over the choice, ought to be ambivalence. The bottle of pills allows full recognition and expression of that ambivalence: I, the patient, can sleep on it, and the pills will still be there in the morning; I do not lose my means of escape through the delay. But if I am terminally ill of cancer in the Netherlands and summon my family physician to my house to administer the fatal dose, I am powerfully motivated to deny any ambivalence I may feel. Wavering at this last minute may forever label me as inconsistent and hence no longer eligible for euthanasia under the official guidelines. Also, I have called the doctor away from his or her family to come to my bedside; I would feel both foolish and impolite were I to change my mind now that he or she has arrived ...

THE LAW

The law cannot reasonably remain indifferent to one person's helping another to die. Presumably, a key goal of the law would be to prevent the risk of abuse. I have insisted on framing assisted death as an exceptional response to medical failure because that framing may by itself go a long way toward preventing the abuses that many legitimately fear. But further protection may come from both legal and professional mechanisms.

I have argued that we do not want an absolute prohibition against physician-assisted death. Neither do we want a nationwide chain of suicide or euthanasia clinics, or a new medical specialty to run them. If the defense of how one has managed a medical failure must occur on a case-by-case basis, we cannot construct a statute that would list all possible justifications and restrictions in advance.

Theoretically, one ought to put legal cases in front of judges and juries. Showing that one acted compassionately and competently in assisting a death, by ensuring that a voluntary choice was made and that all other options for relief had been tried, should constitute a legally acceptable defense against a charge of homicide or assisting a suicide. Experience to date suggests that virtually no U.S. jury would convict in the face of a reasonably persuasive defense of this type, whether the defendant were a physician or a layperson. Certainly, it seems inconceivable that a jury would have convicted Dr. Quill had he been indicted.

Practically, however, the possibility of being called to answer such a criminal charge, with the attendant monetary and publicity costs and the uncertainty of any jury verdict, amounts to a de facto legal prohibition against physician-assisted death. The only feasible solution would seem to be a modification of what now occurs in the Netherlands, where prosecutors have a quasilegal and informal means of deciding not to seek indictments in cases that appear defensible. If panels somewhat like the arbitration boards sometimes recommended to deal with malpractice claims were set up to review cases of assisted death, and if prosecutors agreed that a positive review by the panel suggested a defense that would probably prevail in court, they might be persuaded not to seek an indictment. Such panels, if established, ought to be accompanied by strong penalties against physicians who conceal assistance in death to evade review (as too often happens now in the Netherlands). I specifically recommend that hospital or nursing home ethics committees not be pressed into service as review panels of this type; I think a proper review ought to be more adversarial than these committees ideally are.

This legal framework might be supplemented by intraprofessional review, in an especially rigorous version of the mortality and morbidity conference. Physicians assisting a death should be called on to defend their actions against the sharpest questioning of their peers, in an open forum. If the prosecutors and the general public have faith in the rigor of this peer review, they will be more likely to accept the decision of an arbitration panel and less likely to call for active prosecution under the criminal law for all cases.

The details of this system should be left to legal experts. There is, however, one other condition that humane legal management of assisted death ought to meet. A good death occurs as much as possible among caring and supportive people. If the law forces already suffering patients to die alone – for fear that seeking the supportive presence of others might implicate them in an illegal act – then the law undermines important social values of family and community.

An advantage of this approach to assisted death, for law and public policy, is that the exceptional, hard cases are distinguished from the much more common and less controversial cases. This preserves the distinction between allowing a patient to die by withdrawing or withholding treatment, and causing a patient's death, in those areas of policy where the distinction has the greatest usefulness. Both advocates and opponents of assisted death agree that the distinction between allowing to die and causing death (between passive and active euthanasia) has little if any moral weight. But the distinction has, in the past two decades, proved very useful as public policy, ensuring that qualms about

130

mercy killing and assisted suicide do not override the rights of competent patients or their surrogates to refuse medical treatment. The approach defended here would allow this distinction to remain in force for most cases and would deal with difficult cases, in which the distinction is unhelpful, individually.

CONCLUSIONS

Those on both sides of the debate over assisted death can agree that all patients should be confident that physicians will aid them with the latest palliative care to relieve terminal suffering and will respect their right to refuse life-prolonging treatment and to execute advance health care directives. One hopes that this view, if fully and effectively implemented, would considerably reduce the number of patients who will request a physician's aid in dying.

One also hopes that clearly labeling a good death a medical success will spur a better understanding of the remaining barriers that keep physicians from the appropriate use of palliative measures (persistent beliefs that adequate doses of narcotics will lead to addiction or premature death, for example) and tendencies to deny that the patient is approaching death, so that a switch from life-prolonging to palliative management occurs far too late in the patient's terminal course. Unfortunately, far too many American physicians still think that neglect of symptom control and a "never say die".attitude in the face of worsening illness constitute good medical care. That these instead constitute inappropriate medical practice is a position that must be argued vigorously if the American public is ever to regain the trust in physicians' compassion that we have all too nearly lost.

20 PHYSICIAN-ASSISTED SUICIDE: IDEAS IN CONFLICT

ALWAYS TO CARE, NEVER TO KILL

The Ramsey Colloquium

*The following declaration was produced by the Ramsey Collo-
quium of the Institute on Religion and Public Life in New York
City. The Colloquium is a group of Jewish and Christian theolo-
gians, ethicists, philosophers, and scholars that meets periodically
to consider questions of ethics, religion, and public life. It is
named after Paul Ramsey (1913-1988), the distinguished
Methodist ethicist, who was a pioneer in the field of contemporary medical studies. An abbreviated version of the declaration
appeared in* The Wall Street Journal *of November 27, 1991.*

Points to Consider:

1. Discuss: "Once we cross the boundary between killing and
   allowing to die, there will be no turning back."

2. What is the biblical response of Christians and Jews toward
   dying?

3. How might euthanasia be seen as violating the unalienable
   right to life?

4. How might legalized euthanasia be seen as changing the meaning of medicine?

The Ramsey Colloquium, "Always to Care, Never to Kill: A Declaration on
Euthanasia," **First Things**, February 1992. Reprinted with permission.

We must not delude ourselves. Euthanasia is an extension of the license to kill.

We are grateful that the citizens of Washington State have turned back a measure that would have extended the permission to kill, but we know that this is not the end of the matter. The American people must now prepare themselves to meet similar proposals for legally sanctioned euthanasia. Toward that end we offer this explanation of why euthanasia is contrary to our faith as Jews and Christians, is based upon a grave moral error, does violence to our political tradition, and undermines the integrity of the medical profession.

In relating to the sick, the suffering, the incompetent, the disabled, and the dying, we must learn again the wisdom that teaches us always to care, never to kill. Although it may sometimes appear to be an act of compassion, killing is never a means of caring.

The well-organized campaign for legalized euthanasia cruelly exploits the fear of suffering and the frustration felt when we cannot restore to health those whom we love. Such fear and frustration is genuine and deeply felt, especially with respect to the aging. But to deal with suffering by eliminating those who suffer is an evasion of moral duty and a great wrong.

Deeply embedded in our moral and medical traditions is the distinction between allowing to die, on the one hand, and killing, on the other. That distinction is now under attack and must be defended with all the force available to us. It is permitted to refuse or withhold medical treatment in accepting death while we continue to care for the dying. It is never permitted, it is always prohibited, to take action that is aimed at the death of ourselves or others.

Medical treatments can be refused or withheld if they are either useless or excessively burdensome. No one should be subjected to useless treatment; no one need accept any and all lifesaving treatments, no matter how burdensome. In making such decisions, the judgment is about the worth of treatments, not about the worth of lives. When we ask whether a treatment is useless, the question is: "Will this treatment be useful for this patient, will it benefit the life he or she has?" When we ask whether a treatment is burdensome, the question is: "Is this treatment excessively burdensome to the life of this patient?" The question is not whether this life is useless or burdensome. Our decisions, whether for or against a specific treatment, are to be always in the service of life. We can and should allow the dying to die; we must never intend the death of the living. We may reject a treatment; we must never reject a life.

Once we cross the boundary between killing and allowing to die, there will be no turning back. Current proposals would legalize euthanasia only for the terminally ill. But the logic of the argument – and its practical consequences – will inevitably push us further. Arguments for euthanasia usually appeal to our supposed right of self-determination and to the desirability of relieving suffering. If a right to euthanasia is grounded in self-determination, it cannot reasonably be limited to the terminally ill. If people have a right to die, why must they wait until they are actually dying before they are permitted to exercise that right? Similarly, if the warrant for euthanasia is to relieve suffering, why should we be able to relieve the suffering only of those who are self-determining and competent to give their consent? Why not euthanasia for the suffering who can no longer speak for themselves? To ask such a question is to expose the logical incoherence and the fragile arbitrariness of suggested "limits" in proposals for legalized euthanasia.

We must not delude ourselves. Euthanasia is an extension of the license to kill. Once we have transgressed and blurred the line between killing and allowing to die, it will be exceedingly difficult — in logic, law and practice — to effectively limit the license to kill. Once the judgment is not about the worth of specific lives, our nursing homes and other institutions will present us with countless candidates for elimination who would "be better off dead."

In the face of such mortal danger, we would direct public attention to four interwoven sources of wisdom in our cultural heritage that can teach us again always to care, never to kill.

RELIGIOUS WISDOM

As Christians and Jews, we have learned to think of human life – our own and that of others – as both gift and trust. We have been entrusted to one another and are to care for one another. We have not been authorized to make comparative judgments about the worth of lives or to cut short the years that God gives to us or others. We are to relieve suffering when we can, and to bear with

Cartoon by Mike Ramirez. Reprinted by permission of Coply News Service.

those who suffer, helping them to bear their suffering, when we cannot. We are never to "solve" the problems of suffering by eliminating those who suffer. Euthanasia, once established as an option, will inevitably tempt us to abandon those who suffer. This is especially the case when we permit ourselves to be persuaded that their lives are a burden to us or to them. The biblical tradition compels us to seek and exercise better ways to care. We may think that we care when we kill, but killing is never caring. Whatever good intentions we might invoke to excuse it, killing is the rejection of God's command to care and of his help in caring.

MORAL WISDOM

We may possess many good things in life. Although we benefit from such goods, they do not constitute our very being. We can, if we wish, renounce such goods or give them into the control of another. Life, however, is not simply a "good" that we possess. We are living beings. Our life is our person. To treat our life as a "thing" that we can authorize another to terminate is profoundly dehumanizing. Euthanasia, even when requested by the competent, can never be a humanitarian act, for it attacks the distinctiveness and limitations of being human. Persons – ourselves and others – are not things to be discarded when they are no longer deemed useful...

135

POLITICAL WISDOM

"We hold these truths," the founders of our political community declared, and among the truths that our community has held is that the right to life is "unalienable". All human beings have an equal right to life bestowed by "Nature and Nature's God." Government is to recognize and respect that right; it does not bestow that right.

This unalienable right places a clear limit on the power of the state. Except when government exercises its duty to protect citizens against force and injustice, or when it punishes evildoers, it may not presume for itself an authority over human life. To claim that – apart from these exceptions – the state may authorize the killing even of consenting persons is to give state authority an ultimacy it has never had in our political tradition. Again, legalized euthanasia is an unprecedented extension of the license to kill. In the name of individual rights it undercuts the foundation of individual rights. An unalienable right cannot be alienated; it cannot be given away. Our political tradition has wisely recognized that government cannot authorize the alienation of a right it did not first bestow.

INSTITUTIONAL WISDOM

Legalized euthanasia would inevitably require the complicity of physicians. Members of the healing profession are asked to blur or erase the distinction between healing and killing. In our tradition, medical caregivers have understood this to be their calling: to cure when possible, to care always, never to kill. Legalized euthanasia would require a sweeping transformation of the meaning of medicine.

In a time when the medical profession is subjected to increasing criticism, when many people feel vulnerable before medical technology and practice, it would be foolhardy for our society to authorize physicians to kill. Euthanasia is not the way to respond to legitimate fears about medical technology and practice. It is unconscionable that the proponents of euthanasia exploit such fears. Such fears can be met and overcome by strongly reaffirming the distinction between killing and allowing to die – by making clear that useless and excessively burdensome treatment can be refused, while at the same time leaving no doubt that this society will neither authorize physicians to kill nor look the other way if they do.

CONCLUSION

This fourfold wisdom can be rejected only at our moral peril. By attending to these sources of wisdom, we can find our way back to a firmer understanding of the limits of human responsibility, and of the imperative to embrace compassionately those who suffer from illness and the fears associated with the end of life. Guided by this wisdom, we will not presume to eliminate a fellow human being, nor need we fear being abandoned in our suffering. The compact of rights, duties, and mutual trust that makes human community possible depends upon our continuing adherence to the precept: Always to care, never to kill.

Hadley Arkes, Amherst College; Matthew Berke, *First Things*; Midge Decter, Institute on Religion and Public Life; Rabbi Marc Gellman, Hebrew Union College; Robert George, Princeton University; Pastor Paul Hinlicky, *Lutheran Forum*; Russell Hittinger, Catholic University of America; The Rev. Robert Jenson, St. Olaf College; Gilbert Meilaender, Oberlin College; Father Richard John Neuhaus, Institute on Religion and Public Life; Rabbi David Novak, University of Virginia; James Nuechterlein, *First Things*; Max Stackhouse, Andover Newton Theological School

21   PHYSICIAN-ASSISTED SUICIDE: IDEAS IN CONFLICT

THE CASE FOR RATIONAL SUICIDE

Derek Humphry

Derek Humphry is a leading advocate of physician-assisted suicide and active voluntary euthanasia. He was the founder of the Hemlock Society U.S.A., and his book Final Exit *became a best seller.*

Points to Consider:

1. What is the Hemlock Society's definition of rational suicide?

2. What are the two ethical justifications for autoeuthanasia according to the Hemlock Society?

3. Describe what a person should do to demonstrate that euthanasia is a "considered" decision.

4. Contrast the hospice movement with the euthanasia movement.

5. Comment: "Just knowing how to kill themselves in itself is of great comfort and often extends their lives."

The word "euthanasia" comes from the Greek — eu, "good", and thanatos, "death".

The Hemlock Society is dedicated to the view that there are at least two forms of suicide. One is "emotional suicide", or irrational self-murder in all its complexities. Let me emphasize that the Hemlock Society's view on this form of suicide is approximately the same as that of the American Association of Suicidology and the rest of society, which is to prevent it whenever possible. We do not encourage any form of suicide for mental health or emotional reasons.

We say that there is a second form of suicide, "justifiable suicide" – that is, rational and planned self-deliverance. Put another way, this is autoeuthanasia, using suicide as the means. I don't think the word "suicide" really sits well in this context, but we are stuck with it.

What the Hemlock Society and its supporters are talking about is autoeuthanasia. But we also have to face up to the fact that it is called "suicide" by the law. (Suicide is not a crime in the English-speaking world, and neither is attempted suicide, but giving assistance in suicide for any reason remains a crime. Even if the person is requesting it on the grounds of compassion and the helper is acting from the best of motives, it remains a crime in the Anglo-American world.)

The word "euthanasia" comes from the Greek– eu, "good", and thanatos, "death". But it has acquired a more complex meaning in recent times. The word "euthanasia" has now come to mean doing something, either positive or negative, about achieving a good death.

Suicide can be justified ethically by the average Hemlock Society supporter for the following reasons:

1. Advanced terminal illness that is causing unbearable suffering to the individual. This is the most common reason for self-deliverance.

2. Grave physical handicap, which is so restricting that the individual cannot, even after due consideration and training, tolerate such a limited existence. This is fairly rare as a reason for suicide, despite the publicity surrounding Elizabeth Bouvia's court cases.

WHAT ARE THE ETHICAL PARAMETERS FOR AUTOEUTHANASIA?

1. The person is a mature adult. This is essential. The exact age will depend on the individual.

2. The person has clearly made a considered decision. The individual has to indicate this by such indirect ways as belonging to a right-to-die society, signing a Living Will, or signing a Durable Power of Attorney for Health Care. These documents do not give anybody freedom from criminality in assistance in suicide, but they do indicate clearly and in an authoritative way what the intention was, and especially the fact that this was not a hasty act.

3. The self-deliverance has not been made at the first knowledge of the life-threatening illness, and reasonable medical help has been sought. We certainly do not believe in giving up the minute a person is informed that he or she has a terminal illness, which is a common misconception of our critics.

4. The treating physician has been informed, and his or her response has been taken into account. What the physician's response will be depends on the circumstances, of course, but we advise our members that as autoeuthanasia (or rational suicide) is not a crime, there is nothing a doctor can do about it. But it is best to inform the doctor and hear his or her response. The patient may well be mistaken – perhaps the diagnosis has been misheard or misunderstood. Usually the patient will meet a discreet silence.

5. The person has made a will disposing of his or her worldly effects. This shows evidence of a tidy mind and an orderly life – again, something that is paramount in rational suicide.

6. The person has made plans to exit this life that do not involve others in criminal liability. As I have mentioned earlier, assistance in suicide is a crime. (However, it is a rarely punished crime, and certainly the most compassionate of all crimes. Very few cases ever come before the courts – perhaps one apiece every four or five years in Britain, Canada, and the United States.)

7. The person leaves a note saying exactly why he or she is committing suicide. Also, as an act of politeness, if the deed of self-destruction is done in a hotel, one should leave a note of apology to the staff for inconvenience and embarrassment caused.

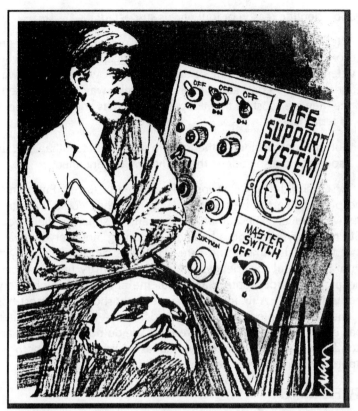

Cartoon by David Seavey. Copyright 1986, **USA Today.** Reprinted with permission.

Some people, because of the criminality of assistance in suicide, do not want to put their loved ones at any risk; such people will leave home, go down the road, check into a hotel, and take their lives.

AUTOEUTHANASIA

Many cases of autoeuthanasia through the use of drugs go absolutely undetected by the doctors, especially now that autopsies in this country have become the exception rather than the rule. Autopsies are performed on only 12% of patients today, compared to 50% in 1965, because of the high cost and the pointlessness of most autopsies. Also, of course, autopsies often catch doctors' misdiagnoses. One study showed that 29% of death certificates did not correlate to the autopsy finding. Many doctors these days prefer not to have an autopsy unless there is good scientific reason or foul play is suspected.

We in the Hemlock Society find that police, paramedics, and coroners put a very low priority on investigation of suicide when evidence comes before them that the person was dying anyway. Detectives and coroners' officers will walk away from the scene, once they are satisfied that the person who has committed suicide was terminally ill.

But, having considered the logic in favor of autoeuthanasia, the person should also address the countervailing arguments:

First, should the person instead go into a hospice? Put bluntly, hospices make the best of a bad job, and they do so with great skill and love. The euthanasia movement supports their work. But not everyone wants a beneficent lingering; not everyone wants that form of treatment and care. Hospices cannot making dying into a beautiful experience, although they do try hard. At best, hospices provide appropriate medicine and care, which everybody deserves. A major study has recently shown that most hospitals have adopted hospice standards, so the hospice movement has done a marvelous educative job. We do not feel there is any conflict of interests between euthanasia and hospices; both are appropriate to different people, with different values.

SUFFERING

The other consideration is this question: Does suffering ennoble? Is suffering a part of life and a preparation for death? Our response here is that if that is a person's firm belief, then that person is not a candidate for voluntary euthanasia; it is not an ethical option. But it should be remembered that in America there are millions of agnostics, atheists, and people of varying religions and denominations, and they have rights, too. We know that a good 50% of the Hemlock Society's members are strong Christians and churchgoers, and that the God they worship is a God of love and understanding. As long as their autoeuthanasia is justifiable and meets the conditions of not hurting other people, then they feel that their God will accept them into heaven.

Another consideration is whether, by checking out before the Grim Reaper calls, one is depriving oneself of a valuable period of good life, and also depriving family and friends of love and companionship. Here again, there is a great deal of misunderstanding about our point of view and what actually happens. Practitioners of active voluntary euthanasia almost always wait to a late stage

142

in the dying process; some even wait too long, go into a coma, and are thus frustrated in self-deliverance.

For example, one man who was probably this country's greatest enthusiast for autoeuthanasia, Morgan Sibbett, had lung cancer. He not only intended at some point to take his life, but he was going to have an "educational" movie made about his technique. I thought the plan was in poor taste myself, and would have nothing to do with it, but it shows the level of his enthusiasm. As it happened, Morgan Sibbett died naturally. He had a strong feeling for life, and he hung on, not realizing how sick he was; then he suddenly passed out and died within a couple of hours. Obviously, he didn't need autoeuthanasia.

My first wife told me her intention to end her life deliberately nine months before she actually did so. When she died by her own hand, with drugs that I had secured from a physician and brought to her, she was in a pitiful physical state; I estimate that she was between one and three weeks from certain death. Her doctor, by the way, when he came to see her body, assumed that she had died naturally – it was that late.

From my years since then in the Hemlock Society, hearing the feedback of hundreds, maybe thousands, of cases, I can assure you that most euthanasists do enjoy life and love living, and their feeling of the sanctity of life is as strong as anybody's. Yet they are willing, if their dying is distressing to them, to forego a few weeks of the end and leave under their own control.

EUTHANASIA

What is also not generally realized in the field of euthanasia is that, for many people, just knowing how to kill themselves in itself is of great comfort and often extends their lives. Once such people know how to make an exit and have the means to do so, they will often renegotiate with themselves the conditions of their dying.

An example quite recently was a Hemlock member in his 90s who called up and told me his health was so bad he was ready to terminate his life. He ordered and purchased the latest edition of *Let Me Die Before I Wake,* Hemlock's book on how to kill oneself, and called back a week or so later to say that he had gotten a friend in Europe to provide him with the lethal overdose. So everything was in position. "Where do you stand now?" I asked cautiously. "Oh, I'm not ready to go yet," he replied. Now that he had the means to make his exit, he was convinced that he could hold on longer. Thus, with control and choice in his grasp, he had negotiated new terms concerning his fate. Surely, for those who want it this way, this is commendable and is in fact an extension rather than a curtailment of life.

A QUADRIPLEGIC LOOKS AT EUTHANASIA

Debbie Lynne Simmons

In the following article, Debbie Lynne Simmons, a quadriplegic, takes a stand for the right to live.

Points to Consider:

1. What dangerous attitude about individuals with handicaps does Simmons see infiltrating our society?

2. Describe the "materialistic ideas" about the value of life that could support euthanasia.

3. What Biblical perspective on the human life is presented here?

4. If euthanasia comes to be viewed as a solution to disability, what may follow?

Debbie Lynne Simmons, "A Quadriplegic Looks at Euthanasia," **The Plough**, March - April, 1985. Reprinted with permission.

We must at no time forget that euthanasia poses an ominous threat to the disabled.

Elizabeth Bouvia admitted herself into Southern California's Riverside General Hospital with the expectation of starving herself to death while the hospital administered pain killers for her arthritis and provided her with hygienic care. A 26-year-old woman struggling with cerebral palsy sought court permission to die.

Shortly after her admission, Elizabeth Bouvia sought legal sanction of her voluntary euthanasia plan. The courts, however, ruled against her, later refusing even to hear an appeal as they upheld the hospital's right to force-feed her. She continued to resist food and defend her position, considering starvation a "natural consequence" of her disability.

Such bitterness is not difficult to understand. Five years after her parents divorced, ten-year-old Elizabeth went into an institutional home for disabled children. At age 17, the girl moved into her own apartment and lived with attendants as she earned her bachelor's degree. She began corresponding with Richard Bouvia while he was in prison and married him after his parole in the fall of 1982. Early in the following year, increasing arthritic pain and financial pressure owing to her husband's inability to find work forced her to quit graduate school. Finally her husband walked out on her, leaving her to blame cerebral palsy for a broken marriage.

Under such circumstances, who can criticize her? Who can say that they wouldn't want to do the same thing if they were in her place?

QUADRIPLEGICS

I believe that my own involvement with cerebral palsy qualifies me to comment. Though we are both quadriplegics, I lack even the minimal hand use that she has. In addition, my speech is garbled, though still intelligible, and I have difficulty swallowing. I do not have arthritis, but the distortion in my frame often causes muscular pain. My need to rely on other people can belittle my sense of independence.

I remember times when I refrained from suicide only to protect my attendant from being implicated. My despondency over my disability usually stemmed from the tremendous improbability of

146

Cartoon by Richard Wright. Reprinted with permission.

marriage caused by my disfigured appearance and physical dependence. At those times the social ramifications of cerebral palsy seemed harder to bear than the physical limitations.

In short, my various struggles with disability help me to sympathize with Elizabeth Bouvia. At the same time, I fear that her proposed voluntary euthanasia reinforces a dangerous attitude slowly infiltrating our society: Individuals with handicaps, from the unborn child to the elderly man or woman, don't really have lives worth living. Already for a number of years, hospitals have quietly allowed defective infants to die under the guise of humanitarian principles.

Elizabeth Bouvia's frequently quoted remark that her condition "is going to keep me from doing the living I want to do" reflects the view that human life derives its value from personal pleasure, convenience, or productivity. In the confines of these materialistic ideas, euthanasia admittedly would be the most reasonable solution to disability.

But the problem extends far beyond human argument. Jesus dealt with the question forthrightly in John's Gospel: "And as he passed by, he saw a man blind from birth. And his disciples asked him, saying, 'Rabbi, who sinned, this man or his parents, that he should be born blind?' Jesus answered, 'It was neither that this man sinned nor his parents, but it was in order that the works of God might be displayed in him.'" (John 9:1-3)

A living illustration of this is a woman I interviewed who has spina bifida. Her birth defect has greatly deformed her legs and made bowel movements uncontrollable. In college she needed a wheelchair to maneuver around campus. Inadequate facilities for disabled students prolonged her education by forcing her to remain on a part-time schedule for several years.

Despite her obstacles, this Christian woman is persuaded that God permitted her disability to accomplish something. She has seen Him use her to give friends a sharper perspective on problems. He has given her a vision of Eternity by teaching her that she has value to Him regardless of her physical condition. She said, "He has shown me that I can be happy, no matter what kind of body I have, because I know Him."

GOD IN CONTROL

My own disability influences nearly every facet of my life, giving me an awareness that God alone is in control. My inability to do things for myself constantly returns me to Jesus, and I'm encouraged by Scripture to believe the Lord took special care in designing me, down to my contracted arms and overactive saliva glands. Psalm 139:14 states, "I will give thanks to Thee, for I am fearfully and wonderfully made." No matter what men think of those of us with physical or mental disabilities, God holds each life to be intrinsically valuable beyond measure. Also, God's ways supersede our own (Isaiah 55:9). Those who embrace euthanasia as a means of minimizing human suffering fail to recognize God's power to redeem such situations.

OMINOUS THREAT

What can be done? As government curtails its assistance to the handicapped in the face of skyrocketing medical care costs, the body of Christ must find alternatives to ensure the handicapped protection. The value of life is confirmed by the willingness of Christians to assume responsibility for those who are unable to take care of themselves.

We must at no time forget that euthanasia poses an ominous

A SPLENDID MESSAGE

In America in 1988, we abort 4,000 children a day, our doctors are into "fetal research", and the warm bodies of dead fetuses are cannibalized for spare parts. At the end of life, we are now being told, "assisted suicide", and "rational suicide", are the reasonable way out for the incurably ill and the very old and very sick. What a splendid message this sends to America's elderly: Why not be reasonable, and move aside, instead of being unreasonable and staying alive?

Patrick Buchanan, "It Is the Right to Die, Or the Right to Kill,"
Conservative Chronicle, November 30, 1988

threat to the disabled, even if it begins as voluntary euthanasia. Once death establishes itself as a solution to the multiple problems that a disability presents, the possibility arises that it will become the definitive solution.

Death is the enemy. No amount of rhetoric, even the most humanitarian, can transform it into a friend.

23 PHYSICIAN-ASSISTED SUICIDE: IDEAS IN CONFLICT

THE DIGNITY IN DECIDING WHEN TO DIE

John Bartholow

John Bartholow is an ecologist with the U.S. Fish and Wildlife Service in Fort Collins, Colorado.

Points to Consider:

1. How successful is hospice care in enabling death with dignity?

2. What are the limitations of drawing up a "living will" and granting power of attorney for health care?

3. Describe "the ultimate personal dignity".

John Bartholow, "The Dignity in Deciding When to Die," **The Baltimore Sun,** 1992. Reprinted with permission.

Most of us trust that we will die peacefully in our sleep at an old age, but frankly, the odds are against it.

My wife Lydia died last June. She had been fighting cancer off and on for 10 years. During that time, Lydia fought bravely to keep living through various complex treatments and their aftermath. As her condition worsened, her last hope was for a bone marrow transplant. She badgered her doctors to "keep the faith."

Finally the doctors told her that there was nothing more they could do. A transplant was no longer possible, and she should expect death soon.

FACING DEATH

Since she was quite uncomfortable, she told her doctors that she was ready to die. She had already lived a full year beyond anyone's expectation.

Would they help her?

No. Legally, there was nothing they could do. Euthanasia was out of the question. It wasn't that they didn't sympathize; it was that euthanasia is against the law – and would jeopardize their careers.

I respected their decision.

When Lydia came home from her last hospital stay, a hospice tried to help. Although the services of the hospice would not prolong Lydia's life, neither would they hasten death. The hospice's idea of death with dignity often means to ease the pain with drugs.

Lydia hated the discomfort, hated the pain, but she hated being drugged even more. I saw no dignity in this kind of chronic sedation. It was then that Lydia asked me to find something to allow her to take her life. Though it turned my stomach, I tried. I contacted the Hemlock Society, which recommended a book, *Final Exit*, by Derek Humphry.

This book graphically described a whole arsenal of techniques, most of which were out of the question as far as I was concerned. Taking hemlock is a painful and uncertain way to die, as are many similar techniques described in the book.

Lydia was now beyond the point where she could actively do

151

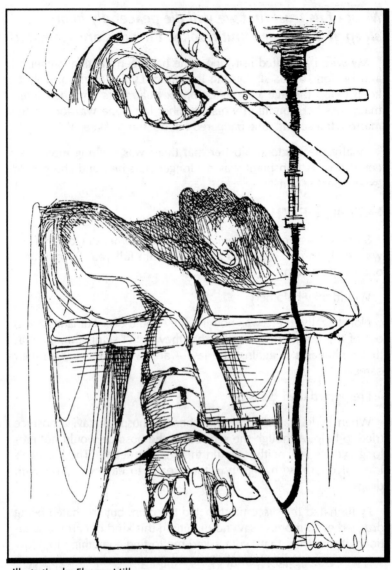

Illustration by Eleanor Mill.

much except swallow a lethal dose of some substance. None of her medication was prescribed in a lethal quantity. Doctors and pharmacists apparently are quite careful to prevent this. In addition, if I were to actively assist in taking her life, I would risk going to jail, leaving our children in a most unsettled state. So Lydia died naturally, but it took seven long days.

THE LAWS

Our laws must be changed so that any patient, in consultation with family, close friends and consulting doctors, may voluntarily choose to terminate his or her life humanely when there is no rational expectation for anything but never-ending misery.

I am not trying to put an additional burden on doctors, but this experience has shown me that they can tell when a situation is hopeless. Hope does not spring eternal, as the saying goes; hope can and does evaporate.

Most of us trust that we will die peacefully in our sleep at an old age, but frankly, the odds are against it. I could tell everyone to be prepared, but few will plan ahead. Arranging for a lethal prescription typically involves deceit, which I cannot advocate. The alternatives, drawing up a "living will" and granting durable power of attorney for health care, are good ideas, but they are fundamentally only requests that people not be treated solely to sustain bodily processes They are not directives. They protect the health-care professionals without really granting rights to the patient.

So changing the law to support self-determination in dying is the only defensible and humane solution that preserves personal dignity.

PERSONAL CHOICE

It matters not to me whether death is an end or a beginning. We should always come down on the side of personal choice. Exercising choice over the time and place of one's death, once death is a certainty and there is no hope, is the ultimate personal dignity. I was disappointed that a "death with dignity" measure was defeated by the voters of Washington State, but similar initiatives will be on the ballot or have been introduced this year in Oregon, California, New Hampshire, Iowa, Maine and Michigan.

For a decade Lydia fought vigorously to live. Why did she have to fight for a week to die? And why should you?

24   PHYSICIAN-ASSISTED SUICIDE: IDEAS IN CONFLICT

EUTHANASIA IS NO PATH TO DIGNITY

Angela Martin

Angela Martin wrote the following article for The Baltimore Evening Sun.

Points to Consider:

1. What relationship does Martin draw between Nazi Germany and euthanasia?

2. Compare / contrast dying with birth.

3. Why might the euthanasia movement be said to be based on fear?

Angela Martin, "Euthanasia Is No Path to Dignity," **The Baltimore Evening Sun**, 1992. Reprinted with permission.

"Death with dignity" is a misnomer. There is nothing "dignified" about death.

Recently my uncle died of cancer. It was not a "good" death. If he recognized the seriousness of his illness, he told no one. He went into surgery expecting to go home after a brief convalescence, but complications developed that required a second emergency procedure.

Afterward he lay in intensive care, surrounded by beeping machines. Though apparently conscious, he never spoke. Nurses assured us he was getting the maximum dose of morphine and felt no pain; but his eyes told a different story. There was no peaceful acceptance there, only pain and fear.

THE VIGIL

And while we kept vigil through endless days, helpless to end his groaning and spasmodic twitching, unable to offer any comfort, we began wishing – praying – for death to come quickly. But death lingered just outside the door, and for two long weeks our lives revolved around his unseeing, unknowing form.

Why? For what purpose? Would not "death with dignity" have been preferable to this useless suffering?

Would it?

At the funeral, a relative criticized his doctor for "keeping him alive." It may have seemed that way to a lay person, but I knew that medical technology had not prolonged his ending.

Yes, he was on a respirator for a few days after the surgery – a conventional practice – but he breathed on his own when it was removed. An IV line delivered fluids to prevent painful dehydration – and also delivered the morphine that, we hoped, kept him beyond the reach of pain. A heart monitor provided information on his condition, but caused no additional discomfort and certainly did nothing to prolong his life.

Sitting in that hospital waiting room, I understood the feelings of those seeking "death with dignity". At the same time, I knew that nothing, short of a lethal injection, could have shortened the dying for my uncle.

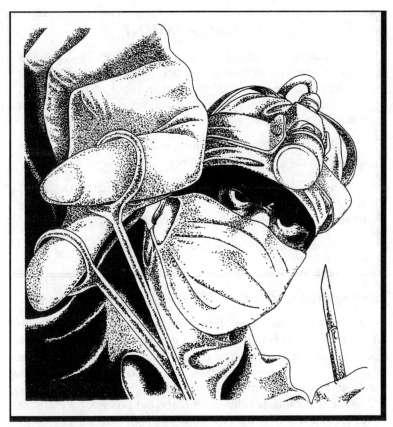

Illustration by Craig MacIntosh. Reprinted with permission from the **Star Tribune**, Minneapolis.

PROPONENTS

Euthanasia proponents prey upon our natural fear of prolonged and meaningless suffering. They have won many converts. But we must think about what euthanasia will do to our society. In Holland, voluntary physician-assisted suicide is permitted but must be reported. A recent study showed that fewer than 10 percent of such "suicides" were reported to authorities, and in many cases, the killing was done without the patient's request or permission.

The Hippocratic Oath was originally devised for the protection of patients. Doctors do, after all, have the power to kill as well as heal. If we allow physicians to kill their patients, where will it end? The complete confidence that once formed the basis of the doctor-patient relationship will be severed. No one will be safe.

We have forgotten how Nazi Germany began its reign of terror. It began not with Hitler, but with a group of German doctors who began practicing euthanasia on the mentally ill and the handicapped. Hitler approved of their euthanasia program, exploiting and extending it to rid the state of other "useless eaters". Today, America is rushing blindly to embrace the philosophy that some lives are not worth living – the cornerstone of Nazi belief.

MEANING OF DEATH

"Death with dignity" is a misnomer. There is nothing "dignified" about death. It is, indeed, the final indignity. But it occurs to me that dying is like birth. We come into this world naked and helpless, prodded and stared at by strangers, unable to exert even the slightest control over the circumstances around us. Even as we struggle against the indignity of it, we realize that the suffering is over. We find that birth is good. We die in the same way, but I'd like to believe that we forget the pain of our dying in the transcendence that follows.

We do not confer "dignity" on our dying by choosing the moment or the means of our final exit, nor do we confer "dignity" on loved ones by killing them. On the other hand, my uncle's painful passage out of this life, ultimately, was filled with dignity. It was seen in the unremitting love of those who surrounded him, valuing his life even as he expelled his last breath.

The euthanasia movement is based on fear. Its proponents offer those who are suffering not the love that casts out fear, only the answer to be found in a bottle of poison. How lonely, how hopeless they must be!

To those who ask "Whose life is it, anyway?" we must answer, "It's not ours." We did not bring ourselves into existence, nor can we claim the power that makes our lives continue. We do not own our lives. We have no right to end them.

25 PHYSICIAN-ASSISTED SUICIDE: IDEAS IN CONFLICT

THE HOSPICE WAY OF DYING

William Lamers, Jr., M.D.

William Lamers, Jr., M.D. is the Medical Director of Hospice of the Canyon in Calabasas, California.

Points to Consider:

1. Describe the philosophy of hospice.

2. What sort of patients are accepted into hospice programs?

3. What trend in the 1940s shifted care from home to hospital?

4. Contrast standard medical treatment for terminal disease with hospice care.

William Lamers, Jr., M.D., "The Hospice Approach," **Choice in Dying News**, Vol. 2, No. 2, Summer 1993. The Newsletter of Choice in Dying - The National Council for the Right to Die (formerly Concern for Dying / Society for the Right to Die).

The hospice approach is simple, but the care involved is not easy.

Hospice is a program of care for dying patients and their families, provided by an interdisciplinary team (nurses, physicians, social worker, aides and others). It is a philosophy, not a place; its goal is to help patients live well while dying. This means refusing the burdens of aggressive life-sustaining treatment, but devoting attention to the effective control of pain.

Most hospice programs care for patients at home, not in a separate facility. The hospice team provides not only physical care, but also social, psychological and spiritual support as needed. Bereavement support is also available for at least a year after the patient's death. Hospice programs accept patients with advanced cancer, AIDS, cardiovascular and neurological disorders and other terminal conditions with short prognoses.

ORIGINS OF THE NEED FOR HOSPICE

Until early this century, most people died at home, cared for by their families and the family doctor. In the 1940s, though, government regulations and health insurance plans shifted the focus of care from the home to the hospital.

At the same time, hospital-based treatment began emphasizing new, aggressive therapies that prolonged existence, but often at the cost of a severely lowered quality of life. Incurable patients were sometimes moved to long-term care facilities where the complex needs of dying persons and their families often were given low priority. New generations facing the death of a loved one were unaware that they could provide excellent care in their own homes.

In the 1970s, hospice programs began to reverse this trend. Today over seventeen hundred hospice programs in the United States enable thousands of persons to receive excellent home care during their last months. If you are considering caring for a loved one in the final phases of illness, the lessons learned in hospice work can benefit you.

PLANNING FOR A HOME DEATH

The hospice approach is simple, but the care involved is not easy. It requires thorough planning and attention to detail.

Whether working with a hospice program or not, anyone planning to bring a patient home to die will need to answer some general questions. Is the patient fully informed of the diagnosis and prognosis? Have reasonable treatment alternatives been considered?

What symptoms are present, and what other symptoms can be

expected in the course of the illness?

Is pain present or anticipated? It is unrealistic to try to care for a dying person at home without excellent pain management. What help does and will the patient need? Who can help provide care twenty-four hours a day, seven days a week for an indefinite period? Do not try to do this alone; you will need support, backup and respite. What medical backup do you have? You will need access at all times to an experienced, cooperative doctor who will make home visits and sign the death certificate.

HOSPICE CARE

The hospice approach to the treatment of the terminally ill focuses on relieving the physical symptoms of patients and on providing psychological and social support for both patient and family. Whereas standard medical treatment for cancer and AIDS patients strives to prolong life at virtually any cost, hospice seeks to optimize the quality of life of the patient's remaining time.

David Cundiff, M.D., **Euthanasia Is Not the Answer**, (Humana Press), 1992

What is the availability of nurses, nurse's aides and LVNs? What social agencies might provide help? Is there a hospice in the community? Check your phone book for the nearest hospice or home health program. What social, psychological, legal, economic and spiritual problems need to be resolved? What personal or family issues might arise? What unfinished business must be completed?

What funeral arrangements have been made? Who should be notified? Have arrangements been made for a doctor to sign the death certificate? What needs will the survivors have after the death? With appropriate support and a good plan of care, caring for a dying person at home can be a uniquely positive, enriching experience.

RECOGNIZING AUTHOR'S POINT OF VIEW

This activity may be used as an individualized study guide for students in libraries and resource centers or as a discussion catalyst in small group and classroom discussions.

Many readers are unaware that written material usually expresses an opinion or bias. The capacity to recognize an author's point of view is an essential reading skill. The skill to read with insight and understanding involves the ability to detect different kinds of opinions or bias. **Sex bias, race bias, ethnocentric bias, political bias** and **religious bias** are five basic kinds of opinions expressed in editorials and all literature that attempts to persuade. They are briefly defined in the glossary below.

FIVE KINDS OF EDITORIAL OPINION OR BIAS

Sex Bias — the expression of dislike for and/or feeling of superiority over the opposite sex or a particular sexual minority

Race Bias — the expression of dislike for and/or feeling of superiority over a racial group

Ethnocentric Bias — the expression of a belief that one's own group, race, religion, culture or nation is superior. Ethnocentric persons judge others by their own standards and values.

Political Bias — the expression of political opinions and attitudes about domestic or foreign affairs

Religious Bias — the expression of a religious belief or attitude

---

Guidelines

1. Summarize the author's point of view in one sentence for each

of the following readings in Chapter Four.

Reading 17 "Assisted Suicide Means Death with Dignity" by Timothy E. Quill, M.D. _____

_____

_____

Reading 18 "The Danger of Legalizing Physician-Assisted Suicide" by Herbert Hendin, M.D. and Gerald Klerman, M.D.

_____

_____

_____

Reading 19 "The Argument for Active Voluntary Euthanasia" by Howard Brody _____

_____

_____

Reading 20 "Always to Care, Never to Kill" by The Ramsey Colloquium _____

_____

_____

Reading 21 "The Case for Rational Suicide" by Derek Humphry

_____

_____

Reading 22 "A Quadriplegic Looks at Euthanasia" by Debbie Lynne Simmons _____

_____

_____

Reading 23 "The Dignity in Deciding When to Die" by John Bartholow _____

_____

_____

Reading 24 "Euthanasia Is No Path to Dignity" by Angela Martin

_____

_____

Reading 25 "The Hospice Way of Dying" by William Lamers, Jr.,
M.D. _____

_____

_____

2. Determine what kind of bias each sentence represents. Is it
   sex bias, race bias, ethnocentric bias, political or **religious
   bias?**

3. Make up one-sentence statements that would be an example of
   each of the following: **sex bias, race bias, ethnocentric bias,
   political bias** and **religious bias.**

BIBLIOGRAPHY

General References

"Always to Care, Never to Kill: A Declaration on Euthanasia." **Current** May 1992: 22-24.

Callahan, D. "The Euthanasia Debate: A Problem with Self-determination." **Current** Oct. 1992: 15-19.

Capron, A.M. and V. Michel. "Be Sure to Read the Fine Print: Will California Legalize Euthanasia?" **Commonweal** Sept. 1992: 16-20.

"Death Potion No. 9." **Time** 1 Feb. 1992: 20+.

Dority, B. "Report from Washington State." **The Humanist** Jan./Feb. 1992: 37-38.

Dworkin, R.M. "Life Is Sacred. That's the Easy Part." **The New York Times Magazine** 16 May 1993: 36.

"Euthanasia Plea Stirs Controversy in Canada." **The Christian Century** 17 Mar. 1993: 288.

Frank, A.W. "Not in Pain, But Still Suffering." **The Christian Century** 7 Oct. 1992: 860-862.

Fuerst, M.L. "Doctors and Suicide." **American Health** Apr. 1993: 25.

Gibbs, N.R. "Mercy's Friend or Foe?" **Time** 28 Dec. 1992: 36-37.

Gibbs, N.R. "Rx for Death." **Time** 31 May 1993: 34-39.

Kass, L. "Suicide." **Commentary** May 1992: 11-15.

McCarthy, J.J. "Physician-Assisted Suicide Shows No Mercy." **U.S. Catholic** Nov. 1992: 14-19.

McCord, W.M. "Death with Dignity." **The Humanist** Jan./Feb. 1993: 26-29.

"Medicide: New Humanism or Old Euthanasia?" **Society** July/Aug. 1992: 4-38.

Morganthau, T. "Dr. Kevorkian's Death Wish." **Newsweek** 8 Mar. 1993: 46-48.

Moroney, E.C. "Three Choices for Death." **America** 21 Nov. 1992: 401-403.

O'Brien, M.J. "Importation of 'Final Exit' Banned in Australia." **Publishers Weekly** 4 May 1992: 14.

"Outlawing Dr. Death." **Time** 8 Mar. 1993: 21.

Pierce, L. "Protests Cause Media Doctor to Cancel Speech." **Christianity Today** 8 Mar. 1993: 58.

Schneider, K.S. "Love Unto Death." **People Weekly** 20 Jan. 1992: 56-60+.

Szasz, T.S. "Death by Prescription." **Reason** Apr. 1993: 46-47.

"There Goes Dr. Death Again: Jack Kevorkian Aids in the Suicide of Another Critically Ill Woman." **Time** 7 Dec. 1992: 29.

Van Biema, D. "Sisters of Mercy." **Time** 31 May 1993: 42-44.

Scholarly References

Barry, Brian. "Suicide: The Ultimate Escape." **Death Studies** Mar.-Apr. 1989: 13, 2, 185-190.

Battin, Margaret. "Voluntary Euthanasia and the Risks of Abuses: Can We Learn Anything from the Netherlands?" **Law, Medicine and Health Care** Spring-Summer 1992: 20, 1-2, 133-143.

Bilimoria, Purushottama. "The Jaina Ethic of Voluntary Death." **Bioethics** Oct. 1992: 6, 4, 331-355.

Byock, Ira Robert. "Final Exit: A Wake-Up Call to Hospice." **Hospice Journal** 1991: 7, 4, 51-66.

Coyle, Nessa; Jean Adelhardt; Kathleen M. Foley; and Russell K. Portenoy. "Character of Terminal Illness in the Advanced Cancer Patient: Pain and Other Symptoms During the Last Four Weeks of Life." **Journal of Pain and Symptom Management** Apr. 1990: 5, 2, 83-93.

Fletcher, Joseph. "The Courts and Euthanasia." **Law, Medicine and Health Care** Winter 1987-88: 15, 4, 223-230.

Glantz, Leonard H. "Withholding and Withdrawing Treatment: The Role of the Criminal Law." **Law, Medicine and Health Care** Winter 1987-88, 15, 4, 231-241.

Glick, Henry R. "The Right to Die: State Policymaking and the Elderly." **Journal of Aging Studies** Fall 1991: 5, 3, 283-307.

Gostin, Larry, and Robert F. Weir. "Life and Death Choices after Cruzan: Case Law and Standards of Professional Conduct." **Milbank Quarterly** 1991: 69, 1, 143-173.

Hollander, Russell; Wolf Wolfensberger; and Louis J. Heifetz. "Euthanasia and Mental Retardation: Suggesting the Unthinkable." **Mental Retardation** Apr. 1989: 27, 2, 53-61.

Jecker, Nancy S. "Giving Death a Hand: When the Dying and the Doctor Stand in a Special Relationship." **Journal of the American Geriatrics Society** Aug. 1991: 39, 8, 831-835.

Loewy, Erich H., and Diane E. Meier. "Healing and Killing, Harming and Not Harming: Physician Participation in Euthanasia and Capital Punishment." **Journal of Clinical Ethics** Spring 1992: 3, 1, 29-34.

Logue, Barbara J. "Death Control and the Elderly." **International Journal of Contemporary Sociology** Jan.-Apr. 1991: 28, 1-2, 27-56.

Logue, Barbara J. "Taking Charge: Death Control as an Emergent Women's Issue." **Women and Health** 1991: 17, 4 97-121.

Madan, T.N. "Dying with Dignity." **Social Science and Medicine** Aug. 1992: 35, 4, 425-432.

Markson, Elizabeth W., and Norman K. Denzin. "Medicide:

New Humanism or Old Euthanasia?" **Society** July-Aug. 1992: 29, 5(199), 4-38.

Martin, Stephen K., and Lillian M. Range. "Extenuating Circumstances in Perceptions of Suicide: Disease Diagnosis (AIDS, Cancer), Pain Level, and Life Expectancy." **Omega** 1990-91: 22, 3, 187-197.

Mizrahi, Terry. "The Direction of Patients' Rights in the 1990s: Proceed with Caution." **Health and Social Work** Nov. 1992: 17, 4, 246-252.

Monte, Philip. "Attitudes toward the Voluntary Taking of Life: An Updated Analysis of Euthanasia Correlates." **Sociological Spectrum** July-Sept. 1991: 11, 3, 265-277.

Pawlson, L. Gregory. "Impact of the Cruzan Case on Medical Practice." **Law, Medicine and Health Care** Spring-Summer 1991: 19, 1-2, 69-72.

Pellegrino, Edmund D. "Doctors Must Not Kill." **Journal of Clinical Ethics** Summer 1992: 3, 2, 95-102.

Raphaely, Den. "Informed Consent near Death: Myth and Actuality." **Family Systems Medicine** Winter 1991: 9, 4, 343-370.

Raudonis, Barbara M. "Ethical Considerations in Qualitative Research with Hospice Patients." **Qualitative Health Research** May 1992: 2, 2, 238-249.

Sampaio, Leonor. "To Die with Dignity." **Social Science and Medicine** Aug. 1992: 35, 4, 433-441.

Teno, Joan, and Joanne Lynn. "Voluntary Active Euthanasia: The Individual Case and Public Policy." **Journal of the American Geriatrics Society** Aug. 1991: 39, 8, 827-830.

Weir, Robert F. "The Morality of Physician-Assisted Suicide. Law, Medicine and Health Care" Spring-Summer 1992: 20, 1-2, 116-126.

Williams, Rory. "Awareness and Control of Dying: Some Paradoxical Trends in Public Opinion." **Sociology of Health and**

Illness Sept. 1989: 11, 3, 201-212.

Zucker, Arthur, and Louise Annarino. "Department of Law and Ethics." **Death Studies** Mar.-Apr. 1989: 13, 2, 207-212.